SAY WHAT'S WRONG AND MAKE IT RIGHT

PROVEN STRATEGIES FOR TEACHING CHILDREN TO RESOLVE CONFLICTS ON THEIR OWN

KAREN TAYLOR-BLEIKER, M.A.

To my dear Charlie, who always encouraged me to Say What's Wrong and Make It Right, especially when he was the recipient.

Cover and interior design by Tabitha Lahr

Published 2019
Printed in the United States of America
ISBN: 978-1-7331145-0-9
E-ISBN: 978-1-7331145-1-6
Library of Congress Control Number: 2019907854

For information, visit www.saywhatswrongandmakeitright.com.

CONTENTS

Introduction vii

PART I—ESSENTIALS OF "SAY WHAT'S WRONG AND MAKE IT RIGHT"

Chapter 1: The Five-Step Process—A Brief Overview 1

Chapter 2: Key Ingredients. 7

Chapter 3: Why the Five-Step Process Works 11

Chapter 4: The Components of a "Caring"
Classroom Environment. 17

Chapter 5: The Components of a "Caring"
Home Environment. 23

Chapter 6: How SWW&MIR Benefits Children 39

Chapter 7: Adult Responsibilities 45

Chapter 8: Assisting Children Who Are Not Ready
to Communicate. 53

Chapter 9: Children as Problem-Solvers 71

Chapter 10: Family and Class Meetings. 81

PART II—FOUNDATION BUILDING

Chapter 11: Framework Activities 119

Chapter 12: Target Lessons for Home and School. 137

Conclusion: "Say What's Wrong and Make It Right"

in Summary 145

APPENDICES

Appendix A: Classroom Lesson Plans 155

Appendix B: Support Materials. 177

Endnotes 201

Bibliography 205

Acknowledgments 211

INTRODUCTION

When I returned to teach kindergarten after ten years teaching third grade, I had forgotten how cute kindergarteners were, how much they stepped on your toes, and how much they tattled. The tattling drove me nuts! That was my original motivation for creating "Say What's Wrong and Make It Right." One secret of the success of this five-step process is that it evolved out of a desire to develop independence in social interactions as well as academic skills in children.

One of my biggest concerns was that many of the same students were coming to me with the same problems day after day. These children weren't exhibiting any growth or progress when it came to handling their difficulties. I felt like I was watching television reruns with no happy endings in sight, and it bothered me that I wasn't making more of a difference. I became increasingly frustrated by this.

The final pieces of the puzzle came together in the classroom. One day, as we were sitting in a circle, one of my students said in a somewhat whiny voice, "Teacher, he's poking me!"

Since I had been seriously working on being more assertive myself for the last few years, my first thought was, *Don't tell me. Tell him.* My immediate second thought was, *This is where assertion training begins.*By spring, because the kindergarteners I'd been teaching to "Say What's Wrong and Make It Right" (SWW&MIR) were displaying such successful problem-solving and communication skills, the principal, my coteacher, and I arranged to teach the process to the first and second grade teachers. We believed that after a few years of teaching these children this five-step process, they would be the best communicators on earth!

Our program was so well received that we went on to teach SWW&MIR to the whole school. Within a few years, this became the accepted way of solving problems throughout the school. Instead of tattling, the worst we teachers heard was the occasional complaint, "I'm trying to talk to Ralph, but he won't talk to me."

At first, SWW&MIR was not taught as a consistent five-step process. It evolved through trial and error. As my partner and I grew in our understanding of how to guide children in solving problems, our students became more successful, and the structure of the process became more consistent. Along with the consistency of the five steps came the strengthening of our belief that children need the opportunity to become more independent and responsible for their growth in social areas, as well as academic areas, from a very early age.

With kindergarteners, I taught SWW&MIR as the need arose from the very first day of school. By the end of

September, the parents and the children knew this was the way we solved conflicts. By December, the kids were solving many problems without my guidance.

In the spring of our third year teaching this process, the video crew from Tustin Unified School District came to film me guiding the children through it. Recess had barely begun when Brian and Tommy became engaged in an obvious disagreement over what they were going to create with the giant jigsaw blocks. They were practically nose to nose, hands on their hips, arguing for their own plan. Snippets of their conversation drifted my way.

"Castle!"

"It's my turn . . . pirate ship!"

"My castle was fun!"

This was the perfect opportunity for me to lead them through SWW&MIR. I casually approached the boys with the cameraman right behind me. I asked, "Is there a problem we need to talk about?"

Both boys responded without missing a beat, "No, we solved it." They were already busy working together to build something.

I was less surprised than the video crew. This was not the first recess I had observed children working out differences on their own.

After another false alarm or two, the district and I agreed to postpone the videoing until fall. It was decided that if we wanted an authentic step-by-step demonstration of my leading the children through the process, we'd have to film at the beginning of the school year, before they had mastered the five-step process.

SWW&MIR is an easy-to-learn process for teachers, counselors, principals, office personnel, parents, grandparents, and child caregivers. It has been gratefully received by all of the above. When I speak to the people to whom I've taught the process over the last thirty years, many of them enthusiastically say they are still using it to this day.

The "Say What's Wrong and Make It Right" process will not end all conflicts and disagreements, but it will:

- Put the responsibility for solving the problem on the people involved.
- Develop communication and other conflict-resolution skills.
- Create an atmosphere of trust and safety.
- Save time and frustration in the long run.
- Phase out your job of being judge, jury, and chief negotiator between children.

This book is for anyone who wants to contribute to developing peaceful communication and problem-solving skills in an individual child, a group of children, or an entire family. Even though this process was developed in a classroom setting and many of the examples you'll encounter in this book take place there, it is totally applicable to any of the aforementioned situations. "Say What's Wrong and Make It Right" as it exists today is based on thirty years of refining and field testing with thousands of children. Parents, teachers, counselors, administrators, aides, and substitutes report the following:

- "Tattling is basically eliminated."
- "Through this talk-it-over process, *both* youngsters see their responsibility in the problem."
- "Students assume responsibility for solving or deterring problems, rather than using physical force."
- "My kids feel so good about handling problems on their own."
- "It takes the adult out of the middle of children's problems."
- "It allows frustrated, angry parents to become observers and active listeners. They learn what really happened rather than a one-sided view."

If the idea of children solving disagreements between themselves appeals to you, read on. Visualize people listening to each other, compromising, and feeling better about themselves—and each other—as a result of their resolving a problem together. Be prepared! Your life with bickering, tattling youngsters is on the verge of drastically decreasing.

PART I

ESSENTIALS OF
"SAY WHAT'S WRONG
AND MAKE IT RIGHT"

CHAPTER 1

THE FIVE-STEP PROCESS—

A BRIEF OVERVIEW

"**S**ay What's Wrong and Make It Right" is based on the belief that children and adults have definite rights and responsibilities in communication and conflict resolution. The following five-step process is easy to learn while building self-esteem:

> **STEP 1:** *Tell the other person you don't like what they are doing.*
> **STEP 2:** *Ask them to STOP.*

These two steps are interchangeable. The order in which they are said is not important. When an individual is upset by something another person is doing, that individual has the right and responsibility to tell the person. If a person is standing on Johnny's foot, Johnny is probably not going to start with saying, "I don't like it when you stand on my foot"; he will probably start with, "Stop standing on my foot!" or "Please get off my foot!" Because of this, these two steps are combined. If a child specifies *exactly* what the other child is doing that upsets him or her, it is less likely to happen again. In fact, once children learn the five-step process, many problems stop here. Too often, an individual assumes others know why she/he is upset. How often have you heard someone say, "He should have known"?

STEP 3: *Tell them your feelings about the situation AND listen to their feelings.*

This is what we call the *heart of the problem*. Our experience has been that when two people who are involved in a conflict state their feelings and perceive that those feelings are being heard, the feelings dissipate—to a degree, at least. Conflicts are not as much about what happened as they are about how the two people *feel* about what happened. Step 3 helps the individuals involved to discover the inner core of the conflict more quickly. If you're facilitating the five-step process, you'll find that problems become solved with greater ease when you remember Step 3. Interjecting, "What are you feeling?" to both parties when they are at a stalemate brings them back to the core issue.

STEP 4: *Tell them what you want them to do to help solve the problem.*

In a conflict, the injured party has the *right and responsibility* to tell the other person what he/she can do to solve the problem. If both have contributed in some way to the problem (as is often the case), this is the time for working out a solution that will make both feel better. Through the talk-it-over procedure in Step 3 and Step 4, children are more likely to recognize and accept their responsibility in the problem. The goal is *solution and growth, not blame.* Because of the above factors *and* because this is taking *their* time, they are more likely to compromise. A frequent request is for the other person to say, "I'm sorry." I never make anyone say they are sorry, because the only thing they are sorry about is that I am telling them to say they are sorry. However, the majority of the time when the two involved in the conflict are looking each other in the eyes, the offender is genuinely sorry and will readily respond with a sincere, "I'm sorry"—without prompting by an adult. On the rare occasion when the offender or one of the offenders has great difficulty saying, "I'm sorry," I usually say something along the lines of, "What else can you do to make you both feel better?" At this point they need to continue dialoguing until they come up with a solution satisfying to both parties.

STEP 5: *Thank them, accept their apology, or compromise.*

This is the time for closure. This is the time for the children to say, "Thank you," "I accept your apology," or "It's okay, if you don't do it again," or to take any other action they have agreed upon. The adult's role is very important here, especially in the first few months, when children are learning to understand the process. The adult facilitator needs to be reasonably certain that both children are feeling fine about the solution they've come up with. If so, the problem is solved. If not, they probably didn't get into what the real upset was about, or they didn't take the time to come up with a solution that was agreeable to both of them. And they will be right back in the problem before the day is over.

The best illustration of this is one of my favorite stories about a student I will call Jeff. It happened on storywriting day many months into the school year. I was busy guiding a group through their individual stories. Jeff came to me from the game center with a tattle about Paul. Before he could explain the problem, I said, "I'll be glad to help you two at recess—unless you think the two of you can work it out on your own right now." I hoped Jeff and Paul were familiar enough with "Say What's Wrong and Make It Right" to go through the process on their own.

I went back to working with my writing group, occasionally glancing toward the problem-solvers to see how they were progressing. Jeff and Paul sat cross-legged on the rug, facing each other, and had an animated dialogue. Soon they came to me declaring that they had worked out the problem. When I asked them both how they were feeling, Paul said, "Fine," and he sounded happy.

Jeff's "Fine!" sounded angry, however.

"You don't sound fine," I said, looking at him. "You sound mad."

By this time he was practically jumping up and down. "I'M NOT MAD!" he shouted emphatically and angrily.

I just sat there smiling at him. In that moment, he finally heard himself.

"It sounds like you two need to talk some more to find out what the problem really is," I said.

By that point, Jeff was starting to grin. He nodded his head in agreement. And off the two of them went to really solve the problem.

CHAPTER 2:

◦———————◦

KEY INGREDIENTS

The following important details *increase the degree and depth of success* the process will have for children and underline the *importance of the facilitator's role* in the beginning stages of training:

1. EYE CONTACT between the parties involved is difficult, but stimulates empathy. I tell students, "Looking in other people's eyes is the path to their hearts." Culturally, this may be strange or uncomfortable for individuals of certain ethnic groups. It is, however, a useful tool in learning how to communicate effectively and resolve conflicts in our Western culture. Recent research indicates that making frequent eye contact is the most intimate thing you can do with another person, and it increases your ability to have an empathetic connection with that person.[1]

2. "I" AND "YOU" ARE PRODUCTIVE COMMUNICATION TOOLS.
Frequently, when children are learning SWW&MIR, they
have a tendency to communicate more with the facilitator
than the other person involved in the conflict. Instead of
using an "I" statement, such as, "I don't like it when I'm
pushed out of the way," *Mary may turn her statement into a
tattle by saying to the adult,* "He pushed me." The facilitator
may need to keep reminding the child, "Don't tell me. Tell
Johnny, 'I don't like it when I'm pushed out of the way.'"
This is an important part of ingredient #3 as well.

3. RESPONSIBILITY belongs to the people involved in the conflict, not the facilitator. Another important part is having
them come up with what they are upset about, what they
are feeling, and what will solve the problem, rather than the
facilitator trying to guess or tell them all of the above. Use
their time, rather than the facilitator's time, when possible.
The level of motivation for solving the problem is usually
increased when children are missing playtime or another
pleasurable activity, rather than taking time away from a
difficult academic task or chore. (Motivation is explained
in greater detail on pages 65–70 in Chapter 8.)

**4. QUESTIONS BEGINNING WITH "WHAT?" RATHER THAN
"WHY?"** invite greater communication. I have learned the
hard way, from experience, that questions like "Why did
you do that?" are door slammers to conversation. *Why?*
questions seem to close down dialogue. There is just something accusatory about "why." Children, often, don't know
why they did what they did. By the same token, questions

such as, "What made you feel like doing that?" or "What do you think caused that to happen?" are door openers. These types of questions help everyone, including the individuals involved in the conflict, gain understanding.

5. BOTH INDIVIDUALS LISTENING TO EACH OTHER shows respect, builds trust, and usually dissipates the upset somewhat. Also, as time goes by this facilitates the process, because both children know they are going to be heard and understand the process will be followed. Knowing the routine increases children's feeling of safety.

CHAPTER 3:

WHY THE FIVE-STEP

PROCESS WORKS

When isn't time an issue for parents and teachers? At home, problems seem to be the most plentiful when you are trying to get everyone out the door on time or you are in a public situation. At school, every year it seems there is more to teach, greater expectations, and a wider range of needs for individual students. And it's *always* on the day when the teacher has the most to squeeze in or the greatest lesson completely ready to be taught that one or two children have an emotional upset.

In *How to Talk So Kids Can Learn*, authors Adele Faber and Elaine Mazlish vigorously encourage spending a few moments dealing with angry or obviously miserable students rather than ignoring them. Ignored feelings don't disappear, they mushroom. Too often, when I've been in the position of having to decide whether to focus on the intense feelings of students or move ahead with my well-prepared plan, I've plowed into the lesson. At some point, an eruption occurs, and ends up taking even more time than I feared in the beginning because the deep feelings were left to fester until they became great enough to stop everything. When I have been astute enough to check in with Tony and Janet to see if they need to "Say What's Wrong and Make It Right," the problem is often solved in two or three minutes. The whole class seems to breathe a collective sigh of relief, and moving forward, the general tone is one of greater trust and safety. In this atmosphere, everyone is much more open to learn the lesson, and I, the teacher, am more able to remain a calm and safe adult.

NIPPING PROBLEMS IN THE BUD

One of the reasons this is true is that anger and fear cause a reactive physiological state that can last for days. In this state individuals are ready to fight, run, throw, yell, and react to a seemingly small provocation at a moment's notice. In his book *Emotional Intelligence*, Daniel Goleman explains that this is why a series of irritants heightens the intensity of reactions. Each upset builds on the previous one. Because of this, it is important for individuals to recognize their feelings and feel safe enough to speak their feelings initially. The sooner upsets are dealt with, the easier it will be for the feelings to dissipate.

One of our kindergarten students, a red-headed little girl, came to school with a new, curly permanent several months into the school year. A few days later, a boy classmate came to me because the girl had kicked him. When I got them together to SWW&MIR, the truth came out. Ever since she had come to school with her curly locks, several different children had called her "Orphan Annie." Instead of saying something the first few times it upset her, she'd said nothing about her distressed feelings. When Johnny called her "Orphan Annie," however, that was the time that did it! She had reached her boiling point, and Johnny was the somewhat innocent receiver of her built-up frustration with all the people that had come before him.

Problems are easier to understand and solve when based on a single incident. In the aforementioned situation, the young girl was upset about a single incident happening repeatedly. But sometimes you encounter an individual who has put up with a series of different upsets throughout the day and failed to assert himself or herself each time, and who eventually has a seemingly unwarranted blowup over a minor irritant. For instance, a day beginning with being yelled at by a family member, followed by being criticized by a boss, called names by a coworker, and being ignored by a friend may be the precursor to stomping out of a meeting with the other participants thinking, *What was that all about?* This is every bit as true on the home front. It is precisely when time is tight and an individual family member (or more) is feeling stressed that emotional eruptions are likely to occur. Taking a few minutes for those who are upset to discuss their feelings usually clears the air and allows everyone's day to start or end in a more peaceful frame of mind.

DEVELOPING INDEPENDENCE IN PROBLEM-SOLVING

Goleman and Growald's "Collaborative to Advance Social Emotional Learning" was based on creating emotionally and physically safe school communities. These environments stimulated and provided for the "four C's: Confidence; Competence; Chances; and Caring."[1] In doing so, student potential for success in academics and potential for emotional growth increased, and the likelihood of social and emotional downfalls decreased. An important contributor to *confidence* is adults treating children as though they are capable of learning, making decisions, and controlling their own behavior.

The reason children don't learn to solve problems on their own is because we as teachers and parents jump in far too soon and do it for them. This loudly shouts, "You aren't capable of solving your problems, so I will do it for you." It deprives children of the *chance* to develop *competency* with problem-solving, as well as to develop the language that is a part of the skill. This jumping in of adults also takes away the children's responsibility and potential for gaining *confidence* in their skill.

Children need guided opportunities—*chances*—to *practice their social skills in order to develop the competencies* that will support and reinforce their *confidence. Too often, adults expect children to use social skills (after a few lessons) with 100 percent mastery, very much like our expectations with Friday spelling tests.* But social skills need an abundance of practice. Even as adults, we don't always show 100 percent mastery in that area.

Finally, a *caring*, supportive, safe environment created by the parents at home or created by the teacher and supported by the school is one where mistakes are to be expected and are all right, children's opinions are encouraged and acknowledged, expectations and boundaries are clear, and everyone is treated with respect. This environment is necessary in order to breed *confidence* and provide the *chances* to practice the social skills needed for the development of *competency* that will nurture and support each child's *confidence*.

DISCIPLINE RATHER THAN PUNISHMENT

Developing a cooperative-based classroom or home rather than one with an authoritarian emphasis diminishes the potential for a power struggle.

The difference between punishment and discipline is that discipline creates growth through respectful treatment of *all*.

Punishment is entangled with blame, shame, and suffering. The emotions children feel after receiving punishment are "resentment, revenge, and retreat into (1) rebellion, (2) reduced self-esteem, or (3) retirement," i.e. complete despair to the point of giving up (Glenn and Nelsen's 2000 description of "Student Reaction to Punishment"). When children are feeling angry, threatened, or depressed, their abilities for thinking, learning, problem-solving, and cooperation become blocked.

WHY SWW&MIR WORKS

In the past, we have thought of reason and emotion as separate entities. The more neuroscientists study how our brains function, the more evidence there is to support how strongly reason and emotion are intertwined. When children are feeling stressed, angry, sad, or fearful, they are less engaged in the learning process. If information signals happiness or opportunity (usefulness), the learner is highly motivated to learn and retains the learning (as discussed by Ruth Palombo Weiss in her 2000 research article "Emotion and Learning"). If Maria's friends Antonio and Janet said she couldn't play in their game during recess, her degree of involvement in solving that problem will be much greater than it is in learning about anything academic. Once the problem is resolved, she will be in a much better state of mind for learning.

CHAPTER 4:

THE COMPONENTS OF A "CARING" CLASSROOM ENVIRONMENT

According to Jane Bluestein's 2001 book *Creating Emotionally Safe Schools,* a "caring" classroom emphasizes establishing a win-win atmosphere for all and eliminating the win-lose structure. The teacher still determines what is and is not negotiable. Students have "power within limits." Boundaries are set with student input into what is helpful to them. Developing responsible, self-disciplined, independent, critical-thinking, cooperative students that act with respect toward others is the goal. The teacher models the behavior expected of students. Conflicts are treated as "problems to be solved rather than battles to be won."

Logical consequences "hold kids accountable without shaming," lecturing, or blaming.

LOGICAL CONSEQUENCES

Logical consequences can be as simple as a child cleaning up the paint he has spilled. Another example is the time my mom had me return money I collected from many neighbors under false pretenses. I was seven, and I went door-to-door, stating that I was collecting for the Red Cross. I actually wanted the money so I could buy a Mother's Day present for my mom. I must have known it was wrong, because I buried the money when I came home. However, my conscience led me to confess to my mom. She calmly said, "No problem. You can return the money to the people." She waited on the sidewalk at each house (and there were several) while I went to their doors, confessed my misrepresentation, and returned their money.

When I tried to return the money to the last donors, they said, "Honey, we didn't give you this much."

I had visions of having to go back to *every* house I had already been to. I pulled myself up as tall as I could and said in a voice as strong as I could muster, "Just take it!" They laughingly took it and shut the door. My mother was none the wiser.

My work was done. However, to this day, it is extremely difficult for me to lie. I know without a doubt, due to that experience, that lying causes you a long city block of trouble.

DEVELOPING COOPERATIVE, EMPATHETIC STUDENTS

Creating an environment in which everyone treats each other with respect involves teaching and encouraging students to:

- Recognize and understand their feelings and the feelings of others (emotional literacy)
- Self-regulate in order to remain calm
- Practice kindness
- Work with others to achieve common goals

Numerous studies have established that emotional literacy improves children's academic achievement and performance, including[1] Goleman (1995), Cummings (1996), and Benson et al (1998). Positive emotional attitudes heighten student motivation to learn and to assume responsibility for learning, as well as for their personal relationships. This increases the teacher's ability to reach and teach students. According to Michele Borba in her 2016 book *UnSelfie,* case after case of recent research further supports the positive role a child's ability to empathize plays in advancing critical-thinking skills and academic test scores. She calls it the "Empathy Advantage." Not only does the Empathy Advantage provide school success, it is a predictor of professional achievement and satisfying relationships in adult life.

THE BENEFITS OF SWW&MIR

The benefits of this process are consistent with the qualities of a "win-win classroom" as described by Bluestein in *Creating Emotionally Safe Schools*. SWW&MIR:

- Supports and thrives in a classroom that encourages children to express their feelings and solve problems responsibly.
- Reinforces learning through teacher modeling and facilitating of the five-step process. Teachers, also, have the right and the responsibility to say when an individual or the class is upsetting them (e.g., "I don't like it when students' eyes, ears, and attention are not on the presenter").
- Provides a forum for hearing and acknowledging strong feelings. This validates students and usually dissipates their upset feelings. It also teaches the valuable nonverbal skill of eye contact.
- Prevents problems. Once students know they have the right and the responsibility to say, "STOP!" when something or someone is upsetting them, many difficulties are avoided. They learn their words are more effective than shoving or hitting.
- Puts the responsibility for solving the problem on the people involved in the dispute. They are motivated to create a solution faster because it is using up their time.

SWW&MIR contributes to a cooperative, responsibility-based classroom, protects student dignity, and creates actual growth—rather than a temporary fix. It assists the teacher in remaining calm and safe to be around, as supported by Carol Bradford Cummings in her book *Managing to Teach*. The teacher's goal during this growth journey is one of facilitator, NOT one of judge, jury, and chief problem-solver. The talk-it-over process provides for Cummings's four areas of growth in problem-solving skills:

- Student recognition of the problem.
- Students understanding and assuming responsibility in their problems.
- Students learning to predict consequences of various solutions.
- Students developing the ability to suggest a better choice for the next time they are in a similar situation.

All of the aforementioned skills create ownership and are more likely to result in follow-through, growth, and increased self-esteem because the thinking and decisions made have come through the students' brains, hearts, and mouths.

CHAPTER 5:

—◦————————◦—

THE COMPONENTS OF A "CARING" HOME ENVIRONMENT

According to Inbal Kashtan in her book *Parenting from Your Heart,* the components of a "caring" home environment are based on the "Power-with" behavioral model rather than the "Power-over" model. "Power-with" includes joint power, collaboration, and finding a way to meet everyone's needs.

POWER-WITH

In the "Power-with" model, Maria is playing house with her younger sister, Jessica. Jessica wants to be the mom because Maria always makes her play the baby. An argument begins. Overhearing this, Mom suggests the use of SWW&MIR:

MOM: Jessica, tell Maria what you're upset about.

JESSICA: I want to have turns being the mom when we play house. I'm tired of always being the baby.

MARIA: But you are the baby in the family.

MOM: Tell each other your feelings and remember to look in the other person's eyes.

JESSICA: It makes me sad when you always make me be the baby and when you say I'm the baby in the family.

MARIA: I'm sorry I make you sad. You make such a good baby. I'm disappointed when I don't get to be the mom.

MOM: Now ladies, what can you do to solve this problem?

JESSICA: We can take turns being the mom.

MARIA: We can both be moms and our dolls can be the babies. Sometimes, Mom, *you* can be the baby.

MOM: That sounds like fun, but I'd like to see that you two cooperate and think about the other person's feelings for one week. When you do that, I'll be happy to take turns being the baby for each one of you. It thrills me to hear you being kinder to each other. So what are you going to do today?

MARIA: Jessica can be the mom today. Tomorrow maybe we'll both be moms to our dolls.

MOM: You are great problem-solvers. I think you will be good mommies. How are you both feeling now?

JESSICA (jumping up and down): Happy!

MARIA: Proud and happy.

MOM (hugging both girls): Me too!

"Power-with":

- Acknowledges and respects all individual family members' feelings and needs.
- Instills behavior expected of children through adult modeling.
- Creates trust and safety, intrinsic motivation, team spirit, and harmony.
- Develops independence, self-esteem, open communication, and empathy.
- Treats conflicts as problems to be solved, rather than battles to be won.
- Results in cooperation, responsibility, joint decision-making, and win-win solutions.

Although the "Power-with" model does take more time initially, the resulting growth and harmony are worth the effort.

POWER-OVER

"Power-over" is the more traditional role of parenting. The emphasis is on the adult's power to control children, "to enforce what the adult wants."

In the "Power-over" model, the scenario starts the same way, with Maria and Jessica arguing about who is going to be the mom this time. When Mom overhears their bickering in this situation, however, she steps in and says, "It makes me sad when I hear you not being nice to each other. If you can't get along, then I guess you make me say, 'No more playing house for one week. If you can cooperate for one week, then you can play house again.' For now, go to your own rooms and figure out another way you can have fun together."

"Power-over":
- Emphasizes the authority figure's feelings, needs, and desires.
- Insists on rule-following and compliance.
- Utilizes coercion, demands, punishment, and rewards.
- Causes guilt, shame, anger, resentment, fear, dependence, and/or loss of self-esteem.

Even though the "Power-over" model takes less time initially, it takes more collective time in the long run because the responsibility remains on the adult. This results in less growth and the return of the same or similar problems.

MAKING POWER-WITH WORK

These definitions are very black-and-white. Parenting is not. Parenthood is the most difficult and important job on this earth, yet often undervalued. At the same time, there are many moments and some days that this overwhelming job can be the most rewarding. In the "Power-with" model, the parent sets boundaries and limits with input from the children where feasible. I've heard people say, "Boundaries and rules are like a big hug." Children are much more comfortable when expectations and limits are established and consistent. Encouraging children's input when establishing rules fosters greater follow-through and cooperation by the children, while the adult's determination of what is and is not negotiable provides security and stability.

Basing decisions on everyone's needs and feelings takes time, empathetic listening, creativity, and compromise. The more parents are able to incorporate these principles in child rearing and communication, the less need there is for punishment, blame, and judgment. The occurrence of a sit-down strike by the child is not as likely.

The outcomes of greater trust, understanding, cooperation, and follow-through are well worth the time and effort. The solutions children come up with and find voice for are the ones they are most likely to follow through with.

At the same time, parents need to have and express clear, consistent boundaries and expectations that create an atmosphere of trust, safety, inclusion, and good hygiene. For example, some of the expectations that work for me are:

- "We wash our hands after going to the bathroom and before eating or food preparation."
- "We use our words and ears instead of our fists for solving problems."
- "We help clean up the messes we make."
- "We tell the truth."

A major concern of all parents is their children's safety. In *You're Not the Boss of Me*, Betsy Brown Braun advises that providing safety while continuing to encourage independence takes time and training. It is important to establish and enforce consistent safety rules and consequences at a young age regarding water, fire, food, traffic, and people. These are a few examples of "Power-with":

- "I will not move this car until all seat belts are fastened."
- "No running in the street. I want you to be safe. If you stay out of the street, we can play ball in the yard. If you go in the street, the game is over. And we will go inside."

If your goal as a parent is to develop caring, responsible, independent, communicative adults, you are probably using many of the tenets of the "Power-with" model. SWW&MIR will support and dovetail into what you are already doing. In order to develop this way of problem-solving between children, and/or adults and children, it is up to adults to lead the way and create an atmosphere that is conducive to learning these skills. Adult modeling will make the difference in the degree of effectiveness. In other words, the more you are able to incorporate these values and methods into your way of life, the sooner you will see an increase in their use by your children.

Many of the "Power-with" components may already be a part of your total family way of life. Most of us see the value of these ideas, but daily schedules, stresses, and our own upbringing send us into automatic reaction mode. In any case, be gentle with yourself. If you gradually add to or change one of the components in your repertoire, you will still see a positive difference. Focusing on small, positive successes in this climate will reinforce your progress. Chastising yourself for slip-ups or mistakes will take you backwards. Your modeling of how to accept mistakes (your children's, your partner's, and your own) as part of the learning, growing process is a huge factor in creating a psychologically safe environment.

RESPECTING AND VALUING ALL FAMILY MEMBERS

Acknowledging and respecting all individual family members' feelings and needs includes accepting verbal expression of feelings by children. A year or two after being introduced to SWW&MIR at our school, a fellow teacher, who was also a young mother, and who understood the value of listening to another's feelings (as well as the fact that feelings aren't "right" or "wrong"), triumphantly shared this story with me:

She went to collect her almost-three-year-old from his babysitter's home, and he met her with, "Want to bite Mommy!"

Instead of taking it personally, she applied empathetic listening by asking, "Are you mad because you wanted to keep playing with Theresa?"

He responded, less emphatically than before, "Yes, want to bite Mommy."

She continued with her empathy. "I understand you're mad about leaving Theresa when you were having so much fun together. But you'll get to play with her tomorrow. It's time for us to go see Grandpa and have dinner."

His anger dissipated because he was heard and understood. He went more willingly with his mother. There was no denial of his feelings and no blame, shame, or punishment for expressing his feelings honestly. She confided that both she and her son felt better at the end of this exchange. Emotional safety was reinforced.

Teaching "emotional literacy" can begin at a young age. "Toddlers understand more than they can verbalize," states Kashtan in *Parenting From Your Heart.* Emotional literacy includes: a personal self-concept; being able to read feelings on another's face; vocabulary to express one's own and others' feelings; the ability to empathize; and the ability to behave in consideration of another.[1] Recognizing and stating a youngster's feelings and needs diffuses a potential power struggle, and it develops emotional literacy.

This type of communication creates and enhances an atmosphere that values and encourages children's verbalization; it encourages them to develop their thinking and learning. This is in direct opposition to the concept that children should be seen and not heard.

The way parents listen to their children and receive their communication (nonverbal as well as verbal) gives them a strong message. Showing respect and value for each individual's opinions, feelings, and needs, especially the need for autonomy, starts with a willingness to be open to varying points of view. Empathetic listening is the perfect vehicle for this. A sincere interest in assisting children with getting in touch with their feelings and needs is necessary. Putting attention on what is going on within children helps us adults avoid taking their messages personally. And according to Marshall B. Rosenberg's 2003 book *Nonviolent Communication,* paraphrasing children's words confirms whether or not they have been heard accurately.

For example, Ralph, a seventeen-year-old, complained at great length to his grandmother about his parents babying his ten-year-old brother. When she realized it was more than complaining, she asked, "Are you worried about his ability to get along in middle school?"

His response was a relieved, "Yes!" She had put into words what his concern was. He felt acknowledged and heard. Also, he gained a greater understanding of why he was upset.

This also works on adults. One twelve-year-old I spoke to was able to listen empathetically when her dad came home from work growling and barking at everyone in sight. Her simple, "What's the matter, Daddy? Did you have a rough day?" let him know that he mattered and was heard (possibly the first time that day). It so soothed him that he was able to stop growling and start acting like the loving father and husband he preferred to be.

In order to be effective empathetic listeners, adults need to be in a place where they can be totally there for the other person. When a dad is not able to because he is still angry about car trouble on the way home, he needs to say so. If a mom is feeling overwhelmed because of an incomplete project that is due at work tomorrow, she needs to speak up. Adults' honest expression of feelings and needs builds trust and safety. Once again, this is modeling the respect and value every family member should hold for each other's feelings and needs.

CREATING THE BEST ATMOSPHERE FOR COMMUNICATION

Cultivating an environment in which good communication takes place involves more than empathetic listening. In *You're Not the Boss of Me*, Braun suggests that other important components include:

- Making sure the television, radio, and all phones are turned off.
- Physical closeness (no large objects, such as a desk, in between the two people).
- Standing or sitting at eye-level with the other person (neither an adult nor a six-foot teenager looking and talking down to the other).

For the "more serious conversations," Braun says, "sometimes it is helpful to plan around something else—a walk, a hike, or a meal out." A mother of three boys contends that her best one-on-one conversations have taken place during snack time or dining out, while her husband treasures the same rapport by taking each boy individually to sporting events.

At my cousin Jim McCullagh's passing, his four daughters enumerated how much they treasured all the ways he spent time with each one of them while they were growing up. High on each one's list was his taking them to sporting events with him individually. This was so important to him that he maintained a posted chart noting when each girl had been his favored guest, and who was next in the rotation. It was not a privilege to be earned; it was each daughter's right as his child, and it's a memory that all four of them cherish to this day.

I am certain that all of these parents would agree with Robert Epstein's science-based research into the "ten most effective child rearing practices." Number one on the list is the support and acceptance of your children, physical affection, and "quality one-on-one time together."

ENCOURAGING AND DEVELOPING INDEPENDENCE AND RESPONSIBILITY IN CHILDREN

When children are encouraged to take responsibility for their actions, they build self-esteem, cooperation, and trust. For this to occur, discipline must be based on logical consequences, with growth, problem-solving, and self-discipline as the goals, as opposed to punishment for the sake of punishment. In *Raising Self-Reliant Children in a Self-Indulgent World*, authors H. Stephen Glenn and Jane Nelsen suggest that exploring what happened together and guiding children in investigating possible solutions and outcomes develops their judgment skills and "their sense of being capable." Let's look at an example: Johnny forgets to take his homework to class, and his parents don't rush to school with it. This is a perfect learning opportunity.

Mom is not surprised when Johnny explodes through the front door with, "Thanks a lot, Mom! Because of you I got in trouble, and I had detention! Why wouldn't you bring me my homework?"

Mom knows that at this point in time, lecturing Johnny about his responsibilities will only fall on deaf ears and infuriate him more. So, in order to assist him in creating his own solution, she chooses instead to give him empathetic feedback, followed by questions to help him solve his own problem. "I'm sorry you got in trouble," she says. "I can see why you're so mad and probably disappointed in me."

"Yeah," Johnny answers—sullenly. But he's also surprised and taken aback by her response.

Mother continues, "I'm so sorry that you're mad and disappointed in me. There are going to be lots of days when I can't come running with your homework. What are some other solutions that would help?"

Still not thrilled, Johnny suggests, "I guess I'm going to have to find a way to remember my homework. I probably need to put it in my backpack when I've finished instead of waiting 'til the next morning."

"Do you think that will work?" Mom asks.

By now Johnny's attitude has lightened up. "Yeah, because everything I have to have is in there. And I always grab my backpack as I walk out the door."

"How does that solution feel?"

Johnny grins. "You're gonna love this . . . It makes me feel kinda grown up."

Mom laughs. "You are right! I do. Also, I love that you were able to solve your own problem."

And if Johnny's solution doesn't work, he's still learned the important lesson that *he*, not his mom, is responsible for and capable of getting his homework to school. He just needs to find the best way to make sure that happens.

SWW&MIR PROBLEM-SOLVING

In order to be effective, problem-solving strategies must emphasize cooperation, compromise, creativity, and teamwork rather than blaming, shaming, or sublimation to authority figures. In his book *Parent Effectiveness Training*, Thomas Gordon says they should also facilitate individuals' problem-solving through empathetic listening and feedback regarding their strong feelings relating to the situation, rather than advice-giving. This opens the door for children to come up with their own solutions while simultaneously acknowledging the value of each person's feelings. When there is ownership in the resolution, follow-through is more likely to happen.

In this process, adults model the behaviors they wish to see in the children they're talking to. Children are great imitators, which is one of their stronger learning tools. If the adults state their feelings and needs, it creates a safe atmosphere for children to do so. However, if parents say, "No toy grabbing!" while snatching a toy to return it to the child who originally was playing with it (in the name of justice and fair play), they are practicing the old adage of, "Do as I say, not as I do."

An example of positive modeling of SWW&MIR by a parent in this familiar scenario might start with the parent saying, "It makes me sad when you grab toys from each other."

PARENT: Johnny, tell Mary how you feel when she grabs your toy from you . . . Remember to look in her eyes.

JOHNNY: It makes me MAD!

PARENT: Mary, tell Johnny what made you feel like grabbing the puzzle.

MARY: Johnny, you ALWAYS play with the doggy puzzle. It's the one I do best.

PARENT: Tell Johnny how you feel when he is always doing the puzzle that you are best at doing . . . Remember to look in his eyes.

MARY: Mad and sad.

PARENT TO BOTH CHILDREN: What can you both do to solve this problem?

This for me is the fun part. It involves the children's hearts and minds. They often come up with solutions I haven't even thought of. Some possible solutions in this situation might be:

- "We can take turns."
- "You can play with it today, and I'll do it tomorrow."
- "We could do harder puzzles together."
- "I'll play with it 'til the big hand on the clock hits 12. Then it will be your turn."
- "Next time you want to play with it, ask instead of grabbing."

Once they've agreed on a solution, it's the adult's place to check on both children's feelings. You can tell by their tone of voice and body language if the problem is solved and they are both feeling better. (See Chapter 1, Step 5 for a reminder of how this may look when the problem is not solved.) If it's not solved, you need to encourage the children to talk some more. This should always be done within the adult's earshot or field of vision so no one is bullied in the talk-it-over process. In this case, the parent could say,

"You don't seem happy with the solution. You need to talk some more until you find a solution that works for both of you. Come in the kitchen while I'm starting dinner so you can work things out." (If you think hunger is part of the problem, a healthy snack may help to move their discussion in the right direction. Many problems are escalated when people of any age are hungry or tired.)

If both people are feeling fine, it's the adult's turn to give specific feedback. For example, "It makes me feel happy and peaceful when I hear you using your words to solve a problem. And I love it that you are being kinder to each other."

At first, adult modeling and facilitating is necessary to teach and reinforce the five-step process of SWW&MIR. It takes time to put the above components into practice. In the long run, however, it saves time, lessens stress, and creates a respectful, communicative, closer family unit.

Many of the benefits of SWW&MIR are consistent with and contribute to the qualities of a "Power-with" home atmosphere. SWW&MIR:

- Encourages and develops independence and personal responsibility.
- Provides a consistent forum for strong feelings to be heard and acknowledged, which often helps to dissipate upset feelings. It also allows for and reinforces the idea that individuals may have varying opinions, feelings, and needs.
- Develops verbal skills in feeling recognition, empathetic listening, and cooperative problem-solving because of its consistency and simplicity.
- Deters difficulties. Once individuals know they have the right and responsibility to say, "STOP!" when something or someone is upsetting, many problems end right there.
- Puts the responsibility for solving the problem solely on the people involved in it.

CHAPTER 6

HOW SWW&MIR BENEFITS CHILDREN

*Promotes growth and independence
in social interaction skills*

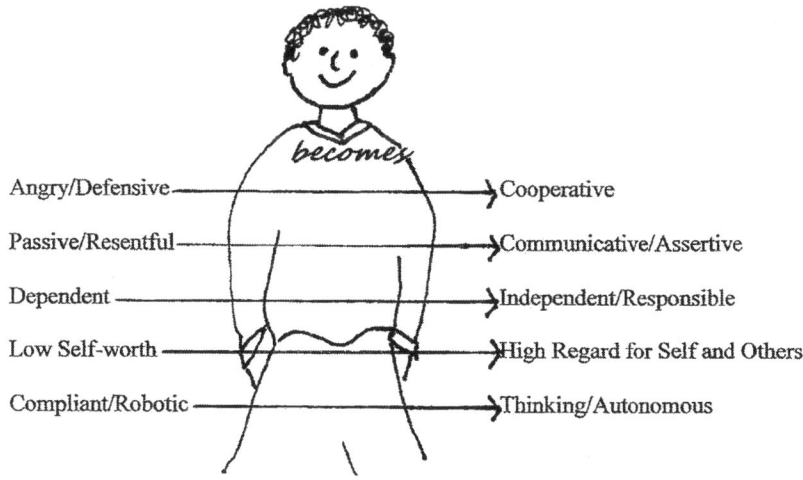

	becomes	
Angry/Defensive	→	Cooperative
Passive/Resentful	→	Communicative/Assertive
Dependent	→	Independent/Responsible
Low Self-worth	→	High Regard for Self and Others
Compliant/Robotic	→	Thinking/Autonomous

TAKES THE ADULT OUT OF THE MIDDLE

PROBLEM PREVENTION

Specific complaints provide insights into what individuals can do to prevent or eliminate problems. When Johnny wanted to play with Ralph, he would come to Ralph and hit him. A fight would ensue. These two third-graders had been in and out of trouble for their fights for some time. Being benched at recess, spending time in the principal's office, notes home, etc. had not curtailed their fighting.

One of their frequent fights happened when I was on recess yard duty. I went with each boy to their respective teachers. I explained that the boys would be spending their next recess in my kindergarten classroom (while I was teaching) in order to resolve their problem.

During my class time, they sat in another part of the room discussing a resolution. When they came to me at the end of their recess time, Ralph and Johnny muttered, through tight lips, "We won't fight anymore." They were still glaring at each other. I envisioned them in another fight before the day was over.

My response was, "You still seem angry. You don't seem to have agreed upon the reason for your fights. Come back to me at your lunchtime so we can get to the bottom of this."

At this point I think they both came to the realization that they might be spending the rest of their recesses throughout the entire school year with me.

When they came back at lunchtime, they were finally ready to "Say What's Wrong and Make It Right."

Johnny started by declaring, "I just punch you to get you to play with me."

Ralph was surprised. He immediately said, "Just say, 'Do you want to play?'"

And that was the end of the problem for the two boys. So much so that they went off arm in arm. This simple resolution pleased both Ralph and me—and, most important, it gave Johnny insight into a more productive way to invite others to play with him.

GROWTH IN SOCIAL EMOTIONAL LITERACY

SWW&MIR's five-step process is a consistent, easy-to-learn formula for daily problem-solving. The children who come to adults to solve their problems throughout the day are given opportunities and guidance in using the process until these communication skills become a part of their repertoire.

LANGUAGE DEVELOPMENT

Children with limited speech and limited English are intrinsically motivated to talk because it is about *their* personal problems and upsets. The simple, consistent script assists them in speaking. As they witness or participate in the five-step process, they learn how safe and satisfying it is.

LESSENING OF ANGER

As strong feelings are stated and heard, they dissipate. Being listened to says, "You matter." As problems are resolved, anger is replaced by calmness, self-worth, pride, connection, and friendship.

SOLUTION RATHER THAN BLAME

Because the goal is solving the problem rather than spending time and energy on who is to blame, the individuals involved accept their responsibility in the problem more readily. Compromise, cooperation, and growth are a direct result.

POSITIVE ALTERNATIVES TO PHYSICAL FORCE

Children experientially learn that talking about the problem is more satisfying and effective than hitting, kicking, pinching, and shoving.

RESPONSIBILITY DEVELOPMENT

When the SWW&MIR's five-step process is the accepted problem-solving method, feelings and needs are expressed and heard. Tattling is virtually eliminated. The responsibility for solving the problem is on the children involved. The adult is no longer judge, jury, and chief problem-solver.

EXPECTED OUTCOMES OF UTILIZING SWW&MIR

- Physical safety of everyone present
- Psychological safety of children and adults
- Ability to recognize feelings and needs of self and others
- Ability to verbalize feelings and needs of self and others

- Adult responsibility in developing communication and problem-solving skills
  - Modeling the skills involved through their own communication with children
  - Guiding the children through the five-step process until the children take ownership
  - Hastening children's learning by consistently using the five-step process in problem-solving situations
- Children take responsibility in communication and problem-solving
  - Saying, "Stop, I don't like this," when upset
  - Using eye contact as a path to another's heart
  - Listening empathetically to create win-win solutions
- Children learn the intellectual concepts upon which SWW&MIR is based
  - Everyone has rights and responsibilities in communication and problem-solving
  - Problems are more about feelings than the event
  - Talking about problems leads to understanding, solution, and empowerment
  - You need to listen to others if you want them to listen to you

CHAPTER 7:

∘———————⊰

ADULT RESPONSIBILITIES

There are five general adult responsibilities that, when applied, will create the optimal conditions for children to learn "Say What's Wrong and Make It Right" and eventually use it on their own, without an adult's presence. These responsibilities are all equally important and in most cases are interdependent:

1. Consistency
- Always follow the same steps.
- Always hear both sides.

2. Availability
- Keep all discussions within earshot.
- Do not step out of the process too soon.

3. Active Listening: Verbal and Body Language
- Know when the problem is not over.
- Ask "what?" questions.
- Offer ideas to keep dialogue flowing.

4. Persistence
- Be sure discussion continues when needed (at snack time, etc.)

5. Neutrality
- Be a guide/facilitator, not a judge or referee.
- Listen to and hear both sides.

1. CONSISTENCY

Always hearing both sides and choosing never to believe one child over another creates great trust. When two children are telling me two different stories (for example, "He started it"; "No, she started it"), my consistent reply is, "I want to believe you both, but you're telling me two different stories. When you have the same story, I will listen to you."

Because the children's physical safety is paramount, their coming up with the same story needs to be done where you can see and/or hear them. With these parameters, no one gets hurt and the truth is more likely to prevail (see "Times and Places to Agree On the Same Story" at the end of this chapter). Often, in this situation, it's the little sweetie pie who never gets in trouble who is trying to shift the blame. If the interaction is with someone that is always in trouble, the sweetie pie is counting on the adult to blame the usual troublemaker. *The adult choosing not to believe one child over the other creates greater trust from both children in the adult and in the value of the problem-solving process.* I have often made a silent bet with myself that sweetie pie, Mary, will prove to be the innocent one, and the majority of the time I've been proven wrong. This may be one of the few times that little Johnny Troublemaker is innocent. Just think what being believed will do for his self-worth and his trust level of adults.

Always following the same steps contributes to quicker and easier mastery. Following the same steps ensures that both parties will be heard. The predictability of the process makes it easier for both parties to listen because both know they will have a turn to be heard.

2. AVAILABILITY

Keep all discussions within earshot or your field of vision. In the process of teaching the children to use their words, we don't want one or both of them getting decked. If one of the children has a tendency to bully or manipulate, this has less chance of happening in earshot of the adult.

Do not step out of the process too soon. You don't have to worry about knowing when to turn the process over to the children. Once they learn it they'll begin using it without your help. By spring I've had a lot of recesses without a tattle.

3. ACTIVE LISTENING

Know when the problem is not over. Watch for dissipation of strong feelings; observe their verbal and body language.

If one or both of the children still appear to be upset, they probably have not touched on the heart of the problem and need to talk some more. Otherwise the problem will reoccur in the near future (e.g., in the next five minutes, two hours from now, tomorrow, and so on).

Offer clues/questions to keep the dialogue flowing. This includes reminding each of the participants to talk to each other when one or both are still turning their statements into a tattle. In the early stage of learning this process, one or both will start with, "He . . ." or "She . . ." My immediate response is, "Tell him/her. Say, 'You . . .'"

The adult may have to do this often at first, until the children become familiar with the idea that they are going to be the ones solving the problem.

When the children are in the early stages of learning the SWW&MIR process, the adult script might go as follows:

ADULT FACILITATOR: (Steps 1 & 2) "Tell the other person what she/he did that upset you and ask her/him to stop." (Make certain that the *Offended Party* is specific about their upset, otherwise the behavior can't be corrected.)

OFFENDED PARTY: Gives a laundry list of complaints.

ADULT FACILITATOR: "What are you the most upset about?" (One complaint at a time, is much easier to address and solve.)

ADULT FACILITATOR: (Step 3) To both individuals, but one at a time, "How did that make you feel?" (At this point, the

Adult Facilitator will probably have to remind the children, "The eyes are the path to the heart. Look each other in the eyes." This, also, stimulates listening to each other.)

ACCUSED PARTY: Has difficulty getting in touch with his/her feelings.

ADULT FACILITATOR: "WHAT made you feel like pushing Johnny?" (Never "WHY?". As discussed in Chapter 2, "what" is a door-opener to communication, while "why" is a door-slammer, because it is often heard as an accusation.) If either party has difficulty naming their feelings, suggest two or three feelings rather than just one. This is more likely to involve thinking rather than echoing on the individual's part.

ADULT FACILITATOR: (Step 4) To the Offended Party, "Say what will make you feel better." (The adult may need to guide choices. Some reasonable, doable requests might be: "Say you're sorry"; "Promise not to do it anymore"; "Play with me"; "Let me in the game"; or "Take turns." Unreasonable requests might be: "Give me money"; "Stay out of my life"; "Eat dirt"; or "Be my slave.")

ADULT FACILITATOR: To the Accused Party, "Can you do that?"

ACCUSED PARTY: "No" (or gives a shrug of the shoulders).

ADULT FACILITATOR: "Then what can you do to make things right?" (If both children have contributed to the problem, as is frequently the case, this is the time for working out a solution that will make both parties feel better.)

OFFENDED PARTY AND ACCUSED PARTY: One or both don't seem able to sincerely do the solution agreed on, *or* one or both still seem upset.

ADULT FACILITATOR: (Step 5) "You need to talk some more. The problem doesn't seem to be solved." (When in doubt, revert back to "What are you feeling?")

4. PERSISTENCE

If the problem doesn't appear to be solved, be sure to find an appropriate time to continue the discussion.

Avoid shortcuts. In the middle of the five-step process, the child that has difficulty dealing with feelings may say, "It's okay." However, it will be good for both children to go through all five steps. In the end, both parties usually feel better. And the more they use the process, the easier and more natural it becomes.

5. NEUTRALITY

Neutrality is essential for the total process. The role of facilitator is that of a guide, not a judge or referee, and especially not a lawyer for one child or the other.

TIMES AND PLACES "TO AGREE ON THE SAME STORY"

As mentioned in Adult Responsibilities, the #1 Responsibility is that of Consistency. Choosing not to believe one child over the other is essential in creating an atmosphere of emotional safety and inclusion. In order to maintain the physical safety of the children and emphasize their responsibility in solving the problem, the two need to talk about what happened in the adult's field of vision or range of hearing. Through this talk-it-over session, they begin to come up with a mutual understanding of the problem situation. There is further motivation to solve the problem because it is taking THEIR time and gaining minimal adult attention. I've listed a few times and places for the children to talk about what happened that should meet the aforementioned criteria.

A. At School:
- During recess, each individual airs his/her view within teacher's hearing (following teachers around, if necessary during their playground duty).
- If it is not settled, use the next recess time.
- Follow the teacher to the office during break, discuss while waiting outside.
- Talk it over quietly near the teacher's desk (while the teacher is working there).
- At a designated "Talk It Over" area of the classroom, each giving their opinions about what happened.

B. At Home:

- In the kitchen, etc., near Mom before watching television, playing, or using the electronics.
- Near Dad while he's washing the car, gardening, etc.
- If hunger is part of the problem, over a snack.
- In the car on the way to or from an activity.
- Always, at the parent's convenience . . . Always BEFORE*

Always before the children can do their own things!

CHAPTER 8:

ASSISTING CHILDREN WHO ARE

NOT READY TO COMMUNICATE

Even after you have established a psychologically safe environment and taught "Say What's Wrong and Make It Right," you will find some children who are not ready to talk it out. These children may be limited in their use of language; they may be English-language learners, shy, speech handicapped, or non-verbal for other reasons. Regardless of the reasons, there are techniques that will assist noncommunicative children to become verbal participants.

Keep in mind that the longer individuals do not speak, the more difficult it becomes for them to talk. That is one of the reasons *family or group recitations of chants, poems, and songs* about strong feelings, including happiness, is a great way to begin. In this way, everyone is included and feels a part of the total group. Risk-taking becomes minimal and everyone can feel successful. In Ron Suskind's book *Life Animated,* he tells the heartwarming story of how his family was able to reach their nonverbal, autistic child, Owen, utilizing Disney film characters' dialogues. The family conversations mimicking those movies stimulated Owen's language and empowered his total development.

NICK

I still remember a particular kindergarten child from my early years of teaching. We will call him Nick. Nick rarely spoke aloud in whole group lessons. When he did, he got red in the face, acted like it was a joke, and struggled to say one or two words. He smiled readily, but it was a nervous, uneasy smile. I later learned he had an angry, demanding father. He probably found it safer and easier to keep his mouth shut at home.

From the first, I knew not to push Nick. When taking attendance, even though I requested that every child answer with at least, "Here," I didn't *demand* it. When I called each name, I would make eye contact and smile at that child. After a few days, all the children were giving at least a feeble "here"—even Nick. On the playground, meanwhile, he was very much a part of everything. He could be seen laughing, talking, playing, running, shouting, and having fun. However, in the classroom, he tended to be nonverbal. His drawing, handwriting, and other written works were haphazard, messy, and almost indecipherable. The work looked like that of a much younger child.

As part of my desire to encourage students, I posted a few student paintings daily; I was careful to keep a record so that everyone's paintings were displayed an equal number of times. One day in late January, I displayed one of Nick's typical paintings. The next day I pointed out his painting on the bulletin board to him. This was not his first painting to be displayed, but it was the first time I had pointed it out to him. He stopped and looked at me as if to say, "You're kidding!" His whole face lit up with a giant smile. Throughout the day, I kept noticing him going over to the display area and staring at his painting.

From that day on his handwriting, drawing, and written work showed dramatic improvement. It was still difficult for him, but he spent more time and put forth much greater effort. There were even times in class when he spoke calmly and with less stress.

The next time he painted, I was the one in shock. The painting was so detailed and colorful, I had to look at the name on the back a second time! Even then I was certain a mistake had been made. By the time Nick confirmed for me that the painting was his, we were both beaming!

IDENTIFY CHILDREN'S STRONG AREA OF INTEREST

This **is** a challenge, but it's crucial. Not only will this help draw out the child, it will also allow the child to forget herself/himself. I focus on children who are limited in language usage in this chapter because how these children are treated is part of creating a psychologically safe learning environment for all. Also, much of what works for the language-limited children works equally well for children who are close-mouthed because of heightened anger, discomfort when dealing with emotions, or a belief that remaining closed-mouthed is the safest bet.

TECHNIQUES FOR ENCOURAGING CHILDREN TO COMMUNICATE

Helping verbally limited individuals find their way to prepare for talking a problem over may be a great challenge. The following techniques are not discussed in progressive order. Any of these can be useful during an actual five-step process talk-it-over when one child is ready to talk and the other child has verbally shut down. This refusal to talk is a sign the child needs time and assistance. These are tools that have proven to be helpful in this type of situation. Each one is not necessarily exclusive. They may overlap and dovetail, depending on the child:

- **RUNNING, OTHER PHYSICAL ACTIVITIES, OR A RELAXATION EXERCISE**, including deep breathing, may be needed for the more physically active child before he or she will be ready to talk. The physical activities suggested in Carla Hannaford's book *Smart Moves* are designed to prepare children for learning at the beginning of the day or the end of recess, but may be helpful on the home front any time an individual needs to refocus.

- **AFTER TALKING TO SOMEONE THEY TRUST** (such as a parent, a teacher, or a peer), some children may be more ready to participate in SWW&MIR.

- **ROLE-WORKING** (as discussed in the section entitled, "Children as Problem Solvers") is another pathway that gives children the opportunity to prepare for the uncomfortable situation in advance by first getting in touch with their feelings. In a safe forum, they are better able to see different ways of handling a problem.

- **DRAWING** is one of the great language liberators. Over the past forty years of my teaching experience, I have seen countless doors open through children's drawings. My master's degree research included interviewing kindergarten students individually regarding their greatest satisfaction during the school day. Five out of six times, the children who were limited in language responded with "drawing," "coloring," or "journal time." Although this was not the major thrust of the research investigation, it was, for me, an eye-opener. My conclusion was, that in order to learn effectively, students limited in language need to experience success through drawing, graphic arts, and eventually writing, because they are limited in the ability to express themselves verbally. Visual representation enables them to communicate with confidence. Socially, it is an equalizer. It invites and allows them to participate in the learning community. This discovery gave me greater understanding and appreciation of these students.

Drawing is also very helpful with the angry children who cannot or will not talk. It gives them a choice of action, and helps them sort out their thoughts and calm down. In *How to Talk So Kids Will Listen & Listen So Kids Will Talk*, authors Adele Faber and Elaine Mazlish share actual examples of parents circumventing potential temper tantrums by providing their children with paper and crayons. When angry, the limbic system closes the pathway to the thinking part of the brain. Drawing, according to Daniel Goleman's *Emotional Intelligence*, helps to dissipate anger by refocusing thinking, and assists the body's physiological state to come back to normal.

As I write this, a kindergartener comes to mind. We'll call him Michael. Michael came in one afternoon roaring like a ferocious beast, ready to lash out at anyone, teachers included. My first question was, "What are you so upset about?" His only response was a very angry, scary glare. I said, in as calm a voice as I could muster, "If you want to stay, you need to draw about what is upsetting you so much so we can help you." I knew I had to redirect him RIGHT AWAY! I also knew that feeling he had a choice, as well as a "cooling off" place, were necessary.

I placed the paper and crayons in front of Michael at a table away from the class. He sat down and furiously started drawing. When he was done, he was calmer. He was still worked up, but he was no longer a scary, ferocious beast. He drew his oldest brother, laughing and large. He drew himself, small and in a dress. As we talked about the drawing, it came out that his brother had put Michael in a dress and made fun of him in front of his teenage friends.

We all were upset for him. You could see it in his class-mates' faces. Some even gave him a soft "Ohhh." I gave him a hug, which he was able to accept. I then gave him some more time alone to draw or look at books until he felt ready to rejoin us. When he came back to the group a few minutes later, he was not bouncing with joy. However, the fury appeared to have dissipated. He was no longer scary or threatening. Many of the children went out of their way to show him kindness with gestures such as a smile or a soft pat on the back. There were no more outbursts from him the rest of the day. The other teacher and I monitored him closely, but he remained safe to be around his classmates.

I cite this story as an illustration of the value of draw-ing as a tool to assist children in dealing with strong feelings and invite cooperation. The end of this story would have been much different if Michael had simply been sent to the principal's office to sit and seethe.

- **WRITING** is a useful tool when older children are acting out or expressing an upset, especially if this happens when there is not time (for example, on the way out the door, in the middle of a lesson, etc.) or willingness on the child's part to talk. A parent might say, "You seem to be upset. Try writing about the problem and possible solutions. Be sure to include anything you can do to help clear up what is bothering you." It helps children see their responsibility in the problem. This is especially true if the adult closes with, "Include what you can do so this is less likely to happen again." Once the children have acknowl-edged their part in their plight, the adult interjecting, "Is there anything the rest of us can do to contribute to the resolution?" reminds them of the support they have from their family or class. It is important for the adult to keep in mind and be clear that this is not a punishment but an avenue to assist the child in her/his quandary.

The same dialogue works as well in the classroom. If students have trouble putting anything down on paper, remind them, "Writing about problems often helps us come up with a solution. You're a good writer. Use your imagination to see what you can do with this." If the child still seems hesitant, suggest, "Try clustering with the problem in the center and brainstorm as many solutions as you can create in five minutes." The words students write are a product of their brains, and they represent their responsibility and choice. Mutual respect and understanding are a direct result. This whole process is much more meaningful and autonomy-building than assigning the child to write a sentence twenty-five times—such as, "I will not shove Jamie"—could ever be. Because of ownership, it is much more likely that the child will show follow-through on the solutions they've written down.

If a student is not ready to respond in writing, some of the aforementioned techniques—physical activity, talking to someone they trust, or drawing—may help them reach the heart of the matter. Remember, the purpose is not to punish but to help them gain understanding.

- **INTERVIEWING CHILDREN ABOUT THEIR AREA OF INTEREST** is a diversionary tactic. It shows respect for individual differences. It is a way of building rapport and calming troubled children—especially angry, language-limited, and shy children. Showing interest in their choice of drawings, games, sports, toys, or books provides an avenue to interview them. Focusing on what excites them (for example, dinosaurs, storybook characters, family fun, trucks and machinery, animals, music, etc.) paves the way for their verbal expression. *Remember: Asking "What?" questions instead of "Why?" questions keeps the conversation door open.*

- **PUPPETS AND DRAMATIZATIONS** of stories about common problems encourage and motivate children that are limited in language usage to speak because they can pretend to be somebody else. They may need the support of your scripting/scaffolding many of the words in order for them to verbalize. This is a safe way to get in touch with and express feelings. The added benefits of hearing themselves speaking, expressing themselves creatively, gaining self-confidence, and feeling part of the group are invaluable. Often, nonverbal children will be motivated to try "Say What's Wrong and Make It Right" with puppets if this is scaffolded for them. Remember 1) to continue to use "I" and "you" statements instead of "she" or "he," and 2) to have the puppets look at and face each other..

Sample Script for Scaffolding and Guiding the Practice

TEACHER TO JUAN: "Have your rabbit puppet say, 'I don't like it when you push me.'" (Include the hand gesture showing pushing.)

JUAN: "I don't like it when . . ."

TEACHER: ". . . when you push me." (Include the hand gesture again.)

JUAN: ". . . when you push me." (Remembers the hand gesture.)

TEACHER: "How did that make your puppet feel?" (Show him pictures or a poster of different feelings.)

Juan points to the sad face.

TEACHER: "Say, 'That made me sad.'"

JUAN: "Bunny sad."

TEACHER TO MARY: "How does your kitty puppet feel? Tell the bunny."

MARY: "Sad and mad . . . I don't like it when you won't listen to me."

TEACHER: "Maybe the bunny and kitty speak different languages. Can you think of a way they can get along?"

MARY: "They can use their motions, like this! Come . . ." (She motions for Juan and his bunny to come, then she and her kitty puppet take the hand of the bunny puppet and Juan.)

TEACHER (clapping): "Great solution! That deserves a silent cheer." (Both hands uplifted as in a cheer with a wide-open mouth, but without a sound.)

TEACHER: "The next time someone doesn't listen to you, Mary, do you think you can try motions like the kitty and you did?" (Act out Mary's motions.)

Mary smiles and nods her head.

TEACHER: "Would you two be willing to do the puppet show for the class so we can show your great solution to everyone?"

If Juan is hesitant, another child will probably be happy to play his part. It should be shared with the class because it will increase understanding among the children and lessen the repeat occurrence of this particular problem.

Often the first words voluntarily spoken to the teacher by students limited in language are through the means of the SWW&MIR five-step process. It is a safe vehicle. They have seen it modeled. They see that both parties are listening, and they go away happier. The language is simple, consistent, and easy to learn. The adult supports those that need it through scaffolding. Because the focus is on actual concerns of the children involved, they are intrinsically motivated. The resulting outcomes are greater self-worth, growth in problem-solving and communication skills, and a greater feeling of inclusion in the class. This encourages the children to use their language even more. Frequently, success through SWW&MIR is the springboard for language growth for these children in many areas of the curriculum.

- **COMBINING DRAWING ABOUT THE PROBLEM WITH INTER-VIEWING** acknowledges the child's autonomy. For the child who is not limited in language or excessively angry, this tool has proven itself useful. This provides children choices when they have backed themselves into a corner by refusing to talk. *(Remember: The longer an individual does not speak, the harder it becomes to talk.)* For example:

TEACHER: "Will you tell me about your picture? Who are these people? What is each one feeling?" (Remember to focus on "What?" questions instead of "Why?" questions.)

BRYAN: "The boy is mad! The girl is sad."

TEACHER: "Bryan, what is he mad about? What is she sad about?"

BRYAN: "The boy is mad because the girl sat in the chair he wanted. The girl is sad because he took the chair away from her."

TEACHER: "What do you think will make both people feel better?"

BRYAN: "If the boy says he is sorry."

TEACHER: "It sounds like you are ready to talk to Jenny. Would you like me to help you?"

Notice that at no time is there a lecture about what Bryan "should" have done.

If this conversation does not go smoothly—if Bryan consistently says, "I don't know," or consistently shrugs his shoulders—this is the adult's cue to suggest, "Maybe Jenny can help us. Shall we go talk to her?" If Bryan is still not ready, he may need to draw some more or try one of the aforementioned techniques. He simply may need to be reassured that he is not in trouble.

MOTIVATING CHILDREN

Motivation for talking about the problem varies with each child. However, in many cases, children are motivated by:

- Being able to use the particular toy or object the conflict is about.
- Being able to play or be friends with the person with whom they were in conflict.
- Being a part of the family or class and doing what everyone else is doing.
- Wanting to connect with and contribute to others.
- Knowing that the main goal is solution, not blame, which builds trust and creates safety.

If the conflict is over a particular toy or object:

- The toy/object may be put away until the family or the class and teacher decide, together, the rules for safe, fair, sharing usage.
- If Melody has been accused by Lizbeth of not following the agreed-upon rules for sharing and safe use of jump ropes and refuses to talk about the problem with Lizbeth, the adult's response might be, "Melody, Lizbeth is trying to talk to you about solving the problem, but you won't talk to her." If Melody has her fingers in her ears and her eyes are closed, the adult can say, "Melody, Lizbeth is going to go back and play until you are ready to talk. Come with me until you are ready to talk. When you are ready to talk, let me know, and we'll have a talk-it-over with Lizbeth. Lizbeth, we will call you as soon as Melody is ready." Melody may need paper and crayons, pencil, or puppets to prepare for her talk-it-over. But she will likely be ready in a matter of minutes, if not seconds, to talk about and try to solve the problem. Playtime and fun are great motivators.

If the conflict is between friends at school or in the neighborhood:

- If Ashley says, "I won't be your friend, Tiffany," and then refuses to talk about it with her, the adult has two courses of action. If Ashley is not present, this is a great opportunity to use the "Active Listening for Feelings" approach explained in Appendix A. For example:

TIFFANY (slamming the door behind her): "Ashley doesn't like me anymore. She doesn't want to play with me or be my friend!"

MOM: "You sound mad."

TIFFANY: "Yeah. I never want to play with her again!"

MOM: "You're so mad you feel like never having anything to do with her."

TIFFANY: "That's right. But then I won't have anyone to walk to school with or play with."

MOM: "You'd miss playing with her and walking to school with her."

TIFFANY: "There's a new girl at school that wants to play with us. I told Tiffany we don't need another friend, but she said we do. Now she's mad at me because I don't want to play with Maria."

MOM: "So Ashley's mad at you because you won't include the new girl."

TIFFANY: "And if I don't, I'm going to be the one left out."

MOM: "Ohhh."

TIFFANY: "I guess I better learn to include Maria. She does seem nice."

MOM: "Do you think including Maria will patch things up with Ashley?"

TIFFANY: "I think so. Can I call her right now and ask?"

- If Ashley is present, the adult may say, "Ashley, Tiffany is trying to talk to you about the reason you are upset with her. Will you talk to her if I help?" If Ashley will respond with why she is upset, the adult will be able to guide the two of them through the SWW&MIR process to a resolution.
- If the conflict is between one individual and a group, it is better to keep the resolution on a one-to-one basis. The more people are involved, the more complicated the problem becomes. It is best for one person to represent the group. Once Ashley and Tiffany have resolved their differences, Tiffany may need to have a talk-it-over with someone else in the group. One-to-one conflicts are more clearly resolved and are fairer than a group against one person.

If the conflict happens during large group or whole class activities:

- Perhaps Bryan has a tendency to use his fists or pushes instead of using his words to communicate. Not talking may have worked for him in the past. He may be afraid of getting into trouble. Using his words, making a mistake, and/or calling attention to himself may be painful for him. An example may be that he pushed Jenny out of the way when he wanted "that" chair. Because of one or all of the above reasons, he refuses to talk to Jenny. If the group is doing something that Bryan is highly interested in, the adult may say, "As soon as you and I have a talk-it-over with Jenny, you may join everyone on the playground."

- Sitting out of the group's activity may not be enough of an impetus for Bryan to talk, especially if any of his reasons for not talking are strongly embedded habits or fears. Drawing about the situation or role-working with puppets may ease his concerns. *He may need to be reminded more than once that he is not in trouble.*

- The way Bryan is treated during his reign of silence is part of reinforcing a psychologically safe environment for all. Whatever choices the adult offers a child, prefacing it with a statement of inclusion such as, "We can have a talk-it-over another day *when you are ready. We are missing you. Are you ready to join us?*" should remind each individual, including Bryan, that everyone's rights and needs are important.

- After exploring all of the above, if there are children that are still tight-lipped, give them time. Until they feel safe, silence is their safety shield. With all the efforts you have made, it will happen . . . and probably when you least expect it.

A WIN-WIN SOLUTION

Through adults' modeling of SWW&MIR and the consistency of the process, everyone will come to know that:

- Every child has input and choices in every situation.
- Each person will be heard.
- The emphasis is on solving problems rather than blaming.
- The process is fair; one child's story will not be believed over the other's. They have to dialogue until they can agree on what happened.
- Completing the process is inevitable.

When working with children, my bottom line is, "Sooner or later we will talk about this and solve the problem." I may not verbalize this, but it is an unspoken agreement I have with myself, especially when at least one of the children seems to be highly upset. Actually, once SWW&MIR is introduced, a punishment-free zone is established. In other words, when we talk about the problem and come up with a solution, no one is in trouble or will be punished—a win for everyone.

CHAPTER 9:

CHILDREN AS PROBLEM-SOLVERS

The outcome of SWW&MIR that may be the most motivating and satisfying to parents and teachers is that children are much more likely to follow through with the solutions that have come from their own brains, hearts, and mouths. I saw this in action when I was substitute teaching.

At the beginning of the day, I elicited from the students the rules that would help them have a good learning day. One of the students pointed out the posted classroom rules. My response was, "I want to hear from *you* what will help you learn best today." The children began suggesting what helped them. Their first two suggestions were 1) a quiet classroom, and 2) time to ask questions when they didn't understand.

When we came to the third rule, Mary raised her hand and said, "Always raise your hand and be called on before talking." My response was, "Great idea!"—especially because the last time I had substituted in this class, Mary had frequently talked out without raising her hand or waiting to be called upon. So I wrote: *3) Always raise your hand and be called on before talking.*

We continued on with two or three more rules. When we were done, our list looked something like this:

> *Our Learning Rules*
> 1. *A quiet classroom*
> 2. *Time to ask questions when we don't understand*
> 3. *Always raise your hand and wait to be called on before talking*
> 4. *Keep your hands to yourself*
> 5. *No making fun of other people or their work*

I posted our rules for the day chart and we began our day. Before too long, you can probably guess who was the first to speak out without raising her hand or waiting to be called upon. This was the exciting part. All I did was hold up three fingers. She giggled and *never* talked out again the rest of the day! What a graphic reinforcement of the value and importance of children coming up with their own rules and solutions.

PROBLEM-SOLVING SESSION

In a fifth grade class, when the need arose or there was a small block of time, we had a Problem-Solving Session. The students wrote their difficulties on 3x5 cards without signing them. I pulled a situation at random out of the basket and read it. The classmates responded to the predicament by suggesting solutions. Often the advice given by children was the very action that would make their life easier if only *they* were to follow it. (This activity would readily adapt to family meetings.)

ROLE-WORKING

This was an even more effective tool used in many of our Problem-Solving Sessions. Calling it role-working instead of role-playing helped the students take it more seriously. (For perfectionists or children fearful of making mistakes, however, calling the activity role-playing can allow them the freedom to relax and be more creative with the activity.)

In these sessions, the fifth graders took turns working/playing the roles of the individual with the problem and the person with whom the child had the difference. They were familiar with the five-step process and the value of including feelings in the discussion. Sometimes, however, the actors came to an impasse and were not solving the problem. When this happened, I froze the actors and:

1. Asked for input—first from the actors about their feelings and thoughts, then from their observing classmates about what they were noticing.

2. Let the actors choose whether to:
   a) continue;
   b) switch roles; or
   c) have other classmates take their places in the role-working.

At the end of the role-working session, we did a debrief where the children discussed what worked best and why. If some were hesitant to express themselves, I'd have them write or draw about it first. This could be followed by having students share with someone near them, and—time permitting—ending with a class discussion or brainstorming of possible solutions. (See a more detailed explanation of brainstorming later in this chapter.)

Role-working gives children the chance to prepare for an uncomfortable situation in advance. It helps them get in touch with their feelings, find out what may or may not work, and develop the language and confidence to SWW&MIR. The switching of roles is especially effective in developing empathy. Role-working can be equally effective on the home front, both in a family meeting or between a parent and a child who is anticipating a confrontation with a friend, schoolmate, or even an adult.

Role-working is especially helpful when preparing a child who is having trouble dealing with a teaser. The standard suggestion is just to ignore the teaser. This is hard to do, however, and is not necessarily effective.

THE DEFLECTING TOOL

There are many ways parents and teachers can help prepare children to deal with teasing. If good-natured teasing, not put-downs, is part of the family or classroom climate, you are already modeling a healthy way of handling it. Your ability to laugh at yourself and your mistakes is excellent modeling for children, according to Betsy Brown Braun.

Teasing can be fun interplay, as long as it's fun for everyone involved, especially the receiver. When it becomes a way to put someone down or cause distress to another, the fun ceases and bullying begins.

Some of the reasons Johnny teases others are because he:

- Is trying to get attention or to connect with others.
- Has been the object of teasing.
- Is trying to make himself feel better by putting others down.
- Likes the reaction teasing incites when he has discovered somebody's sore point (their size, the color of their hair, their name).

Ordinarily I prefer to introduce the Deflecting Tool after children have mastered SWW&MIR. Once the child has mastered the five-step process and used it on the teaser to no avail, it's time to introduce the Deflecting Tool. It is especially helpful if Johnny has discovered Mary's sore spot and won't let up. It can be taught incidentally or as a directed lesson before role-working.

I introduce the Deflecting Tool by likening it to a knight's shield. It's a way to help the tease bounce off you and go in another direction instead of letting it pierce your armor. As a family or class, we brainstorm possible responses that will deflect instead of encourage the tease. Before brainstorming, I share with them some of the following true stories of ways other people have deflected teases successfully:

- Children with a high tolerance for teasing are

able to successfully use responses such as, "So?"; "Whatever"; or "And your point is?"

- Often, positive self-talk leaves the teaser without a comeback. When teased about her clothing, a girl beginning middle school responded with a confident, "Well, that's what's fun about dressing for yourself. I love this outfit!" She walked off with her head held high. She was never bothered by those girls again.

- Upon discovery of Mary's chicken pox during the school day, the nurse had to drive the junior high schooler home. Mary slumped down in the seat opposite her escort and growled, "I hate you, you ol' buzzard you." The nurse responded blithely, "I've thought about being a buzzard. Actually, they have a pretty great life. They are free to fly wherever they want. They have a great view from up high. They don't have to work that hard for their meals. I think it would be great to be a buzzard!" Mary said nothing more, but out of the corner of her eye the nurse could see the girl staring at her. Later on in the school year, when Mary had a more serious problem, it was the same nurse ("the ol' buzzard") whom she respected enough to come to for counseling.

- Penny was a cute, fun, well-liked third grader. The boys in our class were making her life miserable by teasing her about going to a dance with a classmate, Brian. She complained about their teases, stating, "I don't even know how to dance!" My advice was to just say exactly that.

The next time the teasers came gunning for her, she responded with a matter-of-fact, "I don't even know how to dance." When they couldn't get her dander up, they didn't know what to say and that was the end of their teasing.

- Agreeing with the teasers is another form of deflecting. Kenny was a young kindergartener. He had turned five in November just before the December cut-off date. He did not start kindergarten until March. Because of his late enrollment and immaturity, he was not ready to be a successful first grader. Against my advice as his teacher, the parents insisted that he be promoted. In the fall, the first week of school, Kenny's mother came to me to request that he be put back into kindergarten. She said he was coming home every day in tears. I felt that it would be too demeaning by this point, but his mother insisted. When he was reassigned to kindergarten, his first grade classmates started teasing him with, "You're back in kindergarten!" When Kenny responded with a joyful, "Yeah, isn't it great!?" there was nothing left for his would-be teasers to say.

- Twelve-year-old Jimmy complained to me about being teased because he was small for his age. He said when he was teased about his size or anything else, his typical reaction was to get mad. He admitted that it didn't stop the teasers. I suggested that this probably only encouraged them to continue. After I shared some of the above stories, he role-worked with a friend how to deflect a tease. This is a sample of what his Deflection practice sounded like:

TEASER: "You are such a shrimp!"

JIMMY: "Actually, I'm not a Crustacean. I'm a mammal, but I do love shrimp, lobster, and crab. In fact, I think shrimp is my all time favorite. What is your favorite seafood?"

Once he practiced deflecting a few times, he was able to see it as a game. The very next day, when one of his tormentors started in on him, he immediately deflected the tease. The two of them ended up in a friendly conversation, followed by playing a game together. It may be that the teaser was just trying to get Jimmy's attention. Whatever the reason, by deflecting, Jimmy took charge.

After sharing some of these true stories, we brainstorm possible responses to teasers. Then the students take turns trying out responses through role-working of the teaser and the teased. It only takes a short time to see which statements and attitudes are most effective. Having students write an opinion piece about the best way for handling a specific tease reinforces the lesson as well as being a productive form of closure.

BRAINSTORMING

Brainstorming opens the floodgate of creativity and stimulates ownership of solutions in individuals. It is most successful when it is done with a playful attitude. In *Teaching Children to Care,* Ruth Charney instructs her students to "say whatever idea 'pops' into their heads." Often, seemingly crazy ideas are the seed for useful innovations.

Brainstorming may be introduced through a unit of study deciphering what the students already know and what they want to learn about Colonial America, a problem (such as preparing for a test), a small group project, or something as fun as a celebration of the achievement of a class reading goal. Write down every comment without editorializing or reacting in any way. Set a short time limit and stick to it. Five to ten minutes is probably plenty of time. The object is for the children to come up with as many ideas as possible. Usually this calls for two people to write all the ideas on the board or chart papers. When the timer goes off, it's time to look for the ideas that are most helpful and workable.

Brainstorming about the qualities of good friends might include some of the following ideas:

- Letting them copy your work if they're having trouble
- Leaving them alone when they ask you to do so
- Not getting mad at them
- Asking them when you want to borrow something
- Always letting them have their way
- Following the rules of the game (e.g., When you miss the ball, you're out.)

After brainstorming, the children decide together, as a group, which ideas aren't workable. In Jane Nelsen's 2006 book, *Positive Discipline*, she emphasizes the value of posting a sign that reminds students of the "Three R's and an H for Focusing on Solutions (Related, Respectful, Reasonable, and Helpful)." With these rules as a guideline, the children would probably decide to cross the following three items off the list:

- "Letting them copy your work if they're having trouble." (Some of the students will see that this is not helpful or respectful.)
- "Not getting mad at them." (This is not respectful to one's self, and it is not reasonable or helpful in a relationship. If the class is familiar with SWW&MIR, one of the students or the teacher can remind everyone of the value of recognizing and discussing feelings rather than denying or sublimating them.)
- "Always letting them have their way." (This is not reasonable, respectful to one's self, or helpful to the friendship.)

The other three items on the list, in contrast, are all related, respectful, reasonable, and helpful friendship skills.

CHAPTER 10:

FAMILY AND CLASS MEETINGS

I will begin this chapter with specific, step-by-step guide-lines on how to establish the most beneficial family meetings for all the individuals involved. This is vital, because, as Jane Nelsen—the author and coauthor of eighteen books on positive discipline—writes, "Family Meetings are one of the most important tools parents can use to teach children so many valuable social and life skills."

I've devoted the second part of the chapter, meanwhile, to an investigation of the elements needed and benefits derived from successful class meetings. I include experiential stories of the beginning foundation for class meetings in kindergarten, the development of behavior expectations throughout elementary and middle school, the importance and value of the teacher's role, and a detailed exploration of the components needed for an effective, productive interchange.

THE VALUE OF FAMILY AND CLASS MEETINGS

Family and class meetings allow for the development of:

- Critical thinking
- Trust and safety
- Respect and dignity
- Individuals' voices and confidence
- Peaceful solutions

Through:
- Dialogue
- Active listening for feelings
- Collaboration and brainstorming
- Problem prevention and problem-solving
- Dissipating anger
- Cooperation and compromise
- Contribution
- Practice in receiving and giving positive feedback
- Fun and laughter

The above develops feelings of personal significance in the individuals who are included. This is important for many reasons, including the fact that children who perceive themselves as important, contributing members of a family group have greater resistance to peer pressure.[1]

There are many components to successful family and class meetings, according to the abundance of available research. There is general agreement that the value of a meeting is directly related to how safe everyone feels to express their thoughts, feelings, and needs. This is a place for the family or class to solve problems and make decisions as a group, not a place for the adults to establish their rules. The focus is on solutions, not blame.

FAMILY MEETING GUIDELINES: PART I

The guidelines that follow here are not written in cement. Keep in mind the value of family and class meetings mentioned above, and adapt these to what works best for your family. Be flexible. If time passes and an established rule is not working, make changes to continue meeting everyone's needs.

- **REGULARLY SCHEDULED WEEKLY OR BI-WEEKLY MEETINGS** to which everyone is committed have the greatest possibility of being effective. Begin by finding a time that works for everyone. Some suggestions for supporting this commitment include unplugging and turning off phones, as well as placing a "Do Not Disturb" sign on the front door. The meeting should be held in a room with minimal distractions. TV is definitely out. One of the best places is around a cleared dining room or kitchen table.

- **SET A TIME LIMIT AND STICK TO IT.** If four- to six-year-olds are in the family, ten to twenty minutes may be appropriate. Thirty to forty minutes is a good length for older children. Once they hit the teenage years, there may be a need to shorten the meetings or only meet once a month. Each family needs to decide what works for all the family members.

- **DEFINE KEY ROLES.** There are four key roles in a family meeting: leader, secretary, timekeeper, and peace bell monitor. Define their roles clearly for everyone.

  ▶ The **leader**'s role is to guide the group in establishing rules to follow in family meetings, make certain everyone is heard, keep the communication focused on one topic at a time, and explain how the **talking stick** works. The **talking stick** can be any favorite object—a smooth stone, a shell, a heart-shaped beanbag, etc. The only one that speaks at any given time is the person holding the object. Eyes and ears are on the speaker. The listeners are to listen well enough to be able to re peat back the essence of what the speaker said.

  ▶ The **secretary** keeps minutes of agreements reached. If any deadlines or fun activities are scheduled, the secretary may keep a calendar. The secretary may give a summary of the previous meeting at the beginning of next week's meeting.

  ▶ The **time keeper** helps the meeting end on time, times brainstorming sessions, and times any other portion of the meeting that calls for a time limit.

  ▶ The **peace bell monitor** rings a bell to remind the group when there is a need for everyone to take a deep breath. In family meetings, this might be when the issue being discussed brings out strong feelings on both sides. I found this very calming in all of my classes, kindergarten through fifth grade. I taught the children to think, as they were breathing in, *I am calm.* As they were breathing out the thought was, *I am in control.* It helped all of us, me included. I was reminded of what a valuable tool it was when a kindergartener came to me saying, "Teacher, I think we need a deep breath in here."

- **ROTATE MEETING RESPONSIBILITIES.** The adults will need to be the leader and secretary until everyone is comfortable with how the meeting is run. Then even the younger children should have turns at being the leader. When children are treated as if they are capable, they are more likely to see themselves as capable. Once the younger children have the idea of the leader's job, they can be coleaders with an adult. The adult can give support throughout, giving children the words to help them do the leader's job: "Remind everyone to stay on the topic of this year's family vacation" or "Remind them about the talking stick rule."

- **ESTABLISH SAFETY.** Remind everyone that this is a place where each person can express his opinions, needs, and feelings without getting into trouble. One mother reported her children were amazed to find out that Mom and Dad had personal areas they were working on improving. This factor added to the atmosphere of trust and safety the parents were setting out to establish.

  Put-downs, such as "That was a dumb thing to say" or "You don't know how to do anything right," are not allowed. Develop a few more meeting rules that will help maintain a respectful atmosphere. Begin with a discussion of a small problem that is not highly charged or a planning session for a fun family activity, such as a picnic. Robert J. Fetsch and Beryl Jacobson in their Colorado State University Fact Sheet, "Managing Anger Through Family Meetings," suggest that this will make it easier to reinforce the new rules.

- **CREATE AN AGENDA**. This item is number one on Jane Nelsen's list of necessary components of successful family meetings. Family meetings themselves are at the top of her list of "favorite Positive Discipline parenting tools."[2] She contends that a key factor in successful family meetings is to take plenty of time for training all the family members. Her five training components are: "1. The Agenda; 2. Compliments; 3. Brainstorming for Solutions; 4. A family fun activity such as a game, cooking, or popcorn and a movie; 5. Calendar for family fun event."

    Nelsen continues her guidance stressing the details that create a successful foundation.[3] The agenda is where concerns to be discussed are listed. In the first family meeting, this should be the main topic along with establishing guidelines and rules. Elicit from the family members problems they would like on the agenda to be dealt with in the weeks to come. No attempt to solve any problem should be made in the family meeting until the lesson on brainstorming is taught. Let everyone know the agenda will be placed in a prominent place such as the refrigerator. Encourage them to add challenges they want discussed. It may help to write down some the adults have noticed, such as TV or computer time. Subject matter might include chores, responsibilities, privileges, strategies, and consequences.

- **CLOSE ON A POSITIVE NOTE**. Every meeting should "end with something fun that affirms family members," recommend Fetsch and Jacobson. A favorite game or family activity sets the stage and creates anticipation for the family meetings to come in the weeks ahead.

   A mother of two girls told me, "In this day and age of obsession with electronics, the more relational activities yield the greatest potential for creating bonding." Because of this, she prefers games over television or movies. One specific game that is a perfect way to start or end family meetings is a board game called *The Ungame*, created by Rhea Zakich. It is a fun way to increase family communication and build closeness. Through playing this game, family members will:

   - ► Improve listening skills
   - ► Feel safe to express feelings, needs, and ideas
   - ► Gain understanding of themselves and others

There are two levels of questions. Some are light and airy, such as, "What is your favorite gift you've ever received?" Others are more introspective, and are about fears, angers, doubts, and successes. *The Ungame* creates a safe place to express oneself because no one is allowed to interrupt with a comment or question while the person is speaking (which is consistent with the family meeting rules).

Uno is another game that is one of my family favorites. The outcome is always lots of laughter and no hurt feelings because it is all about the luck of the draw, not strategy or competition.

After the family meeting ends, post the list of issues for discussion where everyone can add to it throughout the week. You can remind your children as situations come up, "This might be a good problem for the agenda." Parents also have the right to add disputes that they notice between siblings to the list.

FAMILY MEETING GUIDELINES: PART II

Nelsen suggests that compliments be the main topic for week two of family meetings. The growing agenda should be brought to this meeting. The adult leader should acknowledge that there are quite a few items on the agenda and say something like, "It will be interesting to see how we solve these problems after we learn more about brainstorming. Tonight, though, we are going to learn about compliments."

Compliments can include:

- "Atta boy" or "Atta girl" (acknowledging an accomplishment). The more specific the speaker can be, the better.
  - ▶ "Congratulations on having your painting chosen for the art show."
  - ▶ "Johnny, that was kind of you to give so many of your favorite books to the children's hospital."

- Giving appreciation for something one likes about specific family members is powerful in strengthening relationships.

> ► "It warms my heart to see how quickly you notice ways to help other people. Carrying groceries for Mrs. Martin put a big smile on her face."
> ► "Grandpa, you always listen to me."

- Thanking someone for something they have done for you.
  - ► "Thank you for sharing your Halloween candy with me."
  - ► "Janie, I really liked it when you helped me pick up my things that fell out of my backpack on the way to the bus."

The more specific the compliment is, the more useful the information is for the receiver. Compliments that describe the behavior are more meaningful and reinforce the behavior. Pass the talking stick/object around the family circle and allow everyone to give a compliment. Try to make certain each family member present receives an acknowledgment.

Closing on a positive note for this meeting may include everyone taking turns talking about how receiving a compliment felt.

Children may need to be reminded that put-downs are not allowed. If they are in the habit of bickering or teasing, they may have a tendency to include their gripe with their compliment—for example, "Johnny, I liked it when you helped me with the dishes, but I don't like it when you make fun of my pitching."

If complimenting is difficult for your children, it can be the main part of the agenda again. Or it might be added to the agenda to work on once brainstorming is taught. If the majority of the family does well, brainstorming should definitely be on the docket for the next week.

Throughout the week, when you see possible praise-worthy areas, bring it to the children's awareness with, "That would be a compliment you could give in the next family meeting."

FAMILY MEETING GUIDELINES: PART III

Brainstorming for solutions to problems may be taught in the week three family meeting if the children are beginning to master the ideas of contributing to the agenda and how to give and receive compliments.

Start with compliments, followed by a brief lesson on Brainstorming. Brainstorming can be ideas that are useful or nutty and off the wall. Set a time limit. Two minutes is probably plenty of time. Encourage everyone to come up with as many ideas as possible in the time limit. There are no put-downs; neither should there be a discussion where the ideas are evaluated—not yet. The discussion will come after the timer signals the end of the brainstorming time. The secretary and leader will record all the ideas. Hopefully there will be so many ideas that one person will be unable to do all the writing.

Pick a problem from the agenda (the simpler the better) or a fun family event (perhaps an outing you're planning). Give an example of a ridiculous idea to start the brainstorming. If the problem is "After-dinner clean-up," for example, your ridiculous idea might be, "Pile all the dishes in the sink until we run out of dishes" or "Throw everything in the garbage and buy new dishes at Goodwill."

After brainstorming, use the talking stick/object to select ideas that aren't workable or fair to everyone. Cross those ideas out. This is a perfect place to practice SWW&MIR and the use of "I" messages. From the remaining ideas, the family will choose one idea that everyone is in agreement with. The leader says, "Everyone has agreed to clear their own plates and take their dishes and silverware to the kitchen. Two people will be in charge of cleaning up the kitchen each night on a rotating schedule. The first night will be with an adult and the youngest child. They will make up the schedule for the rest of the week. We will try this idea for one week. Next week, we'll decide if it's a keeper."

Decisions are made by consensus, the general agreement of opinion. If there is an idea with which not every single family member is in accord, the leader says, "We'll table this problem for another meeting to see if we can come up with a solution we all like."

The key is encouraging everyone to have their say. Majority rules or autocratic decision-making defeats the purpose of family meetings. Individual family members who disagree with the majority need to feel that they are heard and that their feelings, needs, and thoughts matter. The object is not to get someone to give in eventually and go along with what most of the family wants; when this happens, the more important results of trust, respect, and inclusion are not being met. Being left out may result in their sabotaging the resolution decided upon. A unanimous verdict, in contrast, incorporates the values of all family members. It increases effective communication, problem-solving, and conflict management, and also dissipates anger.

Keep meetings balanced with happy times and difficulties. One or two problems per meeting is a good limit.

DEBRIEF

Save at least five minutes at the end of each meeting for a debrief, a period when all family members will have time to share their perception of any agreements reached. You may also want to include thoughts and feelings about today's meeting ("I liked it when everybody listened to me. It made me feel proud").

FAMILY FUN AND LAUGHTER

This is an important ingredient in developing community and inclusion. Nelsen suggests that a calendar for fun family events be included once all family members are contributing to the agenda and "doing well with compliments." She recommends planning fun events and putting them on the calendar as a way of ensuring that the family will keep such plans as faithfully as the keeping of dentist appointments.

VIOLENCE PREVENTION

Violence prevention starts in the home. Regularly structured family meetings utilizing the guidelines I've covered in this chapter provide a safe forum for dissipating anger while simultaneously cultivating communication and problem-solving abilities. The long-range effect is the development of social-emotional life skills and greater family harmony.

CLASS MEETING GUIDELINES: PART I

A sense of community is not only a necessary component of successful class meetings, it is also one of the outcomes. Laying the groundwork for class meetings contributes to the psychological and physical safety, trust, and inclusion of everyone. It starts the very first day of school, with each interaction between the teacher and the students as a group. Equally important are interchanges between the teacher and individuals.

Respect, cooperation, and learning thrive in classrooms where the emphasis is on the teachers' relationship to their students, student-to-student relationships, and students' relationship to the curriculum and how they learn best. Students' and teachers' needs, trust, and safety are as important as the curriculum. This is "Power-with" rather than "Power-over," as discussed in Chapter 5. In this atmosphere, studies show improved scores on standardized achievement tests and an increase in ability to learn.[4] Dana Edwards and Fran Mullis, the authors of "Classroom Meetings: Encouraging a Climate of Cooperation," elaborate on the value of classroom meetings, utilizing an abundance of research findings to support their stand that "learning nonviolent ways to resolve conflict is critical in today's world." Classroom meetings with first graders developed their abilities to solve problems on their own and lessened their use of physical and verbal altercations.[5] Utilizing class meetings in middle school and high school on a regular basis contributes to building a "climate of connectedness and belonging," while lessening the potential for bullying and violence. These meetings assist students in generalizing conflict resolution skills to real life. They save time in the long run by decreasing the number and length of disruptions caused by interpersonal conflicts.

In an article about the results of the Child Development Project, Catherine Lewis and her colleagues found that "schools that support caring activities such as cooperative learning, classroom meetings, service projects, and a problem-solving approach to discipline had students who had a strong motivation to learn, increased liking for school, and reduced delinquency and drug use."[6]

William Glasser, in his book *Schools Without Failure*, is a proponent of class meetings with the purpose of helping students with behavior problems. He observed that all students—the whole gamut, from gifted children to children with learning difficulties—became more active learners when they had a voice in classroom management and curriculum. However, before class meetings can be introduced, it is up to the teacher to create a win-win atmosphere for all, with clear boundaries taught and modeled.

When I returned to kindergarten in the late 1970s after ten years teaching third grade, Glasser's theories were becoming widely known and recommended. There was an established kindergarten program in place at my school utilizing UCLA Experimental School teachings and Glasser's theories about the value of class meetings. I entered as a willing learner because I had taught with the lead teacher before. I knew how much she treasured and enjoyed children, and how much she respected their need to explore and have choice. We were highly consistent in philosophy when it came to creating a safe, nurturing environment for all.

The very first day of kindergarten, during the opening moments of class, I was introduced to one of the elements that Glasser would have been delighted to witness. Instead of students sitting in rows or a friendly little group, they were taught how to sit in a circle with the lead teacher, Deedee Carr. As the assisting teacher, I was on the outside of the group, helping to maintain the circle and tending to anyone who was about to cry. For the afternoon class, the same policy was followed, with our roles reversed: I was lead teacher and Carr assisted.

You probably won't be surprised to hear that for at least a few weeks, the circle was not perfect. For many of the children, it was their first time in such a large group. Four- and five-year-olds are not well-known for sitting still. Most of them are not inclined to stay in their own body space. They sit on top of each other, drape themselves over their neighbors, or simply touch, poke, or stroke whoever is next to them. Because of this, we spent our first few weeks in PE class having the children walk around, line up, and do other activities inside of their own hula hoop while reciting, "This is my body space." After a few weeks, most of the children were clear about personal body space.

Listening and waiting for their turn to speak is not always a priority for children. At first, when the teacher says, "Class," "Children," or "Girls and boys," just a few pay attention. Many kids seem to think, *The teacher's not talking to me. She didn't say my name.* Within a month, however, the majority of the students were able to sit and listen with their eyes on the person speaking, stay in their own body space, raise their hand to be called on, or wait their turn for the "talking object" (smooth stone, etc.) to come to them.

We started and ended our day with the whole class circle. We gathered the class together at other times when there was a problem to be solved or a decision to be made, or when we wanted their thinking and input about how to have a successful event, such as a Thanksgiving feast or a school assembly. From the beginning, our kindergarteners were learning they had a voice in their classroom community. It was in this atmosphere that they learned that they had the right and responsibility to "Say What's Wrong and Make it Right."

Various elements go into building the foundation for a successful school year:

- **TAKING AT LEAST SIX WEEKS TO DEVELOP BEHAVIOR EXPECTATIONS** of individuals working in a group, with a partner, and on their own (as is recommended by Ruth Charney in her book *Teaching Children to Care*). This involves teaching routines for use and care of materials, movement from one activity to the next, moving chairs into a circle for a class discussion, and circling up for a game, all of which provide greater chances of success for everyone. For example, I remember being frustrated with Johnny because he seemed to be ignoring the class clean-up routine. Whenever it was clean-up time, he ran to the sink and washed his hands thoroughly while everyone else was on task. I interpreted his hand washing as trying to avoid helping. When I asked him to show me what cleaning up the room meant, he started to go wash his hands again, and I realized that he thought he was doing exactly what was expected. Once I walked him through our routine, he became an enthusiastic leader of making the room spic and span.

- **SITTING IN A CIRCLE** is important because it allows everyone to have eye contact and feel included. It levels the playing field. It is a physical reminder that each individual's opinion is equally important. (Sitting in an oval rather than a circle, in contrast, does not allow every person to have eye contact and be completely included.) Once the circling of chairs has been taught and practiced, it becomes a quick, orderly process.

- **ALLOWING EVERY STUDENT A CHANCE TO SPEAK OR PASS** is a way of reinforcing that everyone's opinions and rights are valued. How this is implemented may vary from teacher to teacher. I've seen this from a variety of perspectives. My personal experience is with five-, eight-, and ten-year-olds. Over time, when given a choice, they spoke when they felt safe enough. If I pressed them to speak before they were ready, it often seemed to stifle rather than encourage them. I am not saying that one way is more correct than another; some teachers believe limited English students will always "pass" if they're not expected to speak. How-ever, the "talking stick" or object encourages the holder to at least say, "I pass," or "Come back to me later." This is another way of reinforcing that everyone is to listen to the speaker and everyone has a turn.

The level of participation and thinking is greater by all when students are seated in a circle, whether the discussion be about the cause of the Westward Movement, sharing personal strategies for a new math concept, or any other subject. In *Building Classroom Discipline*, authors C. M. Charles and Gail Senter discuss how leading authorities advocate the importance of valuing student input into their learning. When they establish the rubric for the assignment to be turned in, their motivation to do well is increased, because it is seen as their choice rather than as a demand from an authority figure. This creates ownership, empower-ment, and consequently greater interest. Equally important is the learners' understanding of expectations. Because they have grappled with the language and details of the rubric, their perception of the task is much clearer.

Charney teaches expectations through explaining, modeling, and demonstrating. She follows her teaching by providing opportunities for students to practice and try out the rules and skills she has just taught. She vividly remem-bers being afraid to volunteer answers for fear of being wrong when she was a child. Because of this, she continu-ally strives to create an atmosphere of safety for every child. Instead of chastising a child for making fun of another's incorrect answer, she makes statements to the class such as, "It takes courage to speak when you don't feel so sure. I want this to be a class where everyone feels they can contribute . . . their sure things and their not-so-sure things. We learn more when we make mistakes."[7] This type of statement models encouragement, consideration, and kindness.

A statements such as, "It makes me sad when I hear someone making fun of someone else," models "I" messages and paves the way for teaching SWW&MIR. Demonstration of how it feels to be listened to—or not listened to—through role-working (see Chapter 9) is a more powerful and lasting way to teach social skills. Charney sets up the situation to demonstrate how people feel when they are not listened to. As soon as the speaker starts looking discouraged, the teacher stops the role-working and elicits responses from the other children about how the speaker must be feeling. Asking for the students' input on how we can make the person speaking feel good and want to talk is much more likely to inspire good listening than a lecture or list of good listening rules, especially when it's followed by more role-working around good listening.

CLASS MEETING GUIDELINES: PART II

Another important step in developing community is having the whole class participate in creating rules. This sets the stage for class meetings. It creates empowerment. Also, there will be greater follow-through from all students because the rules have come through their brains, hearts, and voices.

In his book *Beyond Discipline: From Compliance to Community*, Alfie Kohn asserts, "Students coming together to reflect on how they can live and learn together is the difference between being prepared to spend a lifetime doing what one is told and being prepared to take an active role in a democratic society."

The approaches to establishing classroom rules are varied. The key is making certain that the children know that every person's input is valuable. The purpose is to ensure an atmosphere of safety and peace for everyone. As such, these rules need to be stated in a positive manner. For example, you might phrase one rule as "Only one person may talk at a time" instead of "Don't talk when someone else is talking."

Keep in mind that the fewer rules there are, the easier it will be for your students to follow them.

Some things to keep in mind regarding class rules:

- **SOME RULES NEED TO BE ESTABLISHED RIGHT AWAY**, especially in primary grades, to enforce some semblance of order as the school year begins. Some helpful tools are: songs, poems, and finger plays; a freeze signal; a talking stick or object; visual signs, such as ears for listening and eyes as a reminder to look at the speaker; and verbal recognition when students are learning to follow the rules. For example, "Nearly everyone is listening and looking at Johnny while he is talking. How does that make you feel, Johnny?"

- **INTRODUCE "SAY WHAT'S WRONG AND MAKE IT RIGHT" INCIDENTALLY BEFORE TEACHING IT FORMALLY.** Before I ever go through the formal introduction of SWW&MIR's

five-step process with students, I introduce it incidentally. The first day of school, I lie in wait for a tattle. Usually it happens within the first few minutes of recess. My response is usually, "Have you told the other person?" The talebearer often looks at me as if to say, "Why would I want to do that?" But they verbalize a reluctant "no." To this I say, "Talk to Mary. Tell her what you're upset about with her. If she won't listen to you, come back and I'll help you work it out with her." This is my informal way of introducing the children to the idea that they can solve their own problems. I send the tattler off, but keep the child in my field of vision and within hearing distance. As always, everyone's physical safety is the priority.

- **INVOLVE A CLASS IN WRITING A "BILL OF RIGHTS" OR "CONSTITUTION" CAN HELP ESTABLISH A SAFE AND DEMOCRATIC CLASSROOM.** This is particularly effective for fifth grade through the middle school grades. As Chris Byron, a middle school teacher-researcher, explains, "Equality and justice emerge . . . as key issues when students decide that everyone should have the right to be treated equally, listened to, and to state their ideas without being laughed at."[8] This is not a process that can be hurried. Byron's class's "Bill of Rights," with her guidance evolved into "several months of drafting, discussing, categorizing, and revising" guidelines for how they would live as a community. This may seem like a long time; however, the value of lessons learned and heightened sense of inclusion the students got out of this process far outweighed the amount of time they invested in it.

In an interview, Byron said that some of the main abilities the students gleaned from their class meetings were verbalization, question-asking, problem-solving, evaluating, synthesizing learning, and, generally, thinking more critically. In an atmosphere where everyone feels safe to speak and is expected to participate, quiet kids blossom. Everyone's voice is respected.

- **THE TEACHER'S FUNCTION IS THAT OF A GUIDE.** Appropriate behavior is established through questioning the group about what encourages them to feel safe to contribute. All opinions are accepted. No "put-downs" are allowed. The adult is the role model, as well as a non-judgmental participant. The teacher asks questions to stimulate thinking and for clarification rather than to offer edicts or reinforce personal beliefs. Open-ended questions cannot be answered with a "yes" or "no." Some examples of thought-provoking questions are:

  ▶ What is your best way for learning new information or a new skill?
  ▶ What problems or concerns do you have with this assignment? What might be helpful to you as you try to complete it?
  ▶ What are the possible reasons for this person's actions?
  ▶ What surprised you? What did you notice or learn?
  ▶ How do you feel about this? What do you think causes that feeling?

► What could we do to change this or make a difference?

After conducting a class discussion about rules the students had found useful in the past, Debby Roth told her third graders they would be participating in rule-making for their class. They compared rules starting with "Don't" with rules stated in a more positive manner. It was decided that their class rules would be stated positively. After several days of discussing and playing with wording, their homework assignment was to write one rule that was important to them.

The students' rules were listed on a chart. The teacher had rules she felt were important on a second list. For several days they discussed all the rules until all agreed upon the rules that would help everyone have a great year.[9]

When these approaches to rule-writing are implemented in the classroom, the students come to know the importance of their voice. Because they have a say in establishing class rules, they have more buy-in. They are willing to take responsibility for following *their rules*.

CLASS MEETING GUIDELINES: PART III

Once a win-win classroom has been introduced and reinforced, class meetings support the sense of community while deepening everyone's learning and ability to resolve conflicts. Because of this, the minutes and hours spent in class meetings save time in the long run.

The guidelines for class meetings that I'm presenting here are based on research and personal experiences.

In reality, there are probably as many variations on these guidelines as there are individual teachers. However, there are certain ones that increase a class's probability of success—for example, the idea that the teacher should be a guide/facilitator rather than a dictator. Glasser refers to this type of teacher as a "lead teacher" as opposed to being a "boss teacher."[10] Nelsen, meanwhile, contends that class and family meetings based on "cooperation, mutual respect, and focusing on solutions" are the most important contributors to developing numerous "social and life skills," including the qualities of ". . . a sense of belonging and significance, self-discipline, cooperation, responsibility, resilience, resourcefulness, and problem-solving skills."[11]

The "lead teacher" is objective and non-judgmental, and asks open-ended questions in order to encourage critical thinking and problem-solving. Questions beginning with "What" or "How" stimulate student thinking, show acceptance, and invite input. Lecturing, moralizing, using the word "should," or asking, "Why did you do that?" do just the opposite.

In an article in *Democracy & Education*, Chris Byron describes her weekly class meetings with her sixth graders, and how she sees her role as that of facilitator and guide. In the particular meeting she describes in the article, the students are discussing power and "power relationships" in their school. Sam has just proclaimed that eighth graders don't bully him. He assures Tom, a smaller boy in the class, that he will take care of him if the eighth graders give him trouble. Sam turns to Scott, another student, and says, "Sorry Scott, I can't help you because you do things to upset people." At this, Byron poses the question, "So you mean it's okay for the eighth graders to beat up Scott?" Then everyone has opportunity to comment upon the topic at hand—in this case, the question of "unfairness." There may not be an immediate solution in this class meeting, but student interest, critical thinking, and learning are definitely taking place. And it won't be the end of discussing power and unfairness.

Jane Nelsen's book *Positive Discipline* has many suggestions for and keys to creating successful class meetings. She gives six main reasons class meetings fail. From these negatives, it is easy to imply six positive keys to successful class meetings:

- Meet in a circle.
- Pass a talking stick or other object around the circle in order for every student to speak and be heard.
- Have meetings on a regularly scheduled basis.
- Be a "lead teacher," not a "boss teacher."
- Teach students non-punitive problem-solving skills, such as SWW&MIR, including "I" messages, engaging in active listening for feelings, brainstorming, and role-working before beginning class meetings.
- Have faith in their abilities.

If the goal is to empower everyone, meeting in a circle and passing a talking stick levels the playing field. Both show respect and inclusion of every individual and each person's opinion. They are physical reminders that the class as a whole will be working together to solve problems.

A couple more ways to ensure class meeting success are:

- **SCHEDULING MEETINGS ON A REGULAR BASIS.** This regularity acknowledges their importance. Charney advocates meeting once a week at the same time, with allotments of thirty minutes for third through fifth graders, and forty-five minutes for sixth through eighth graders. Edwards and Mullis also suggest forty-five minutes for high schoolers. (These time allotments may be unrealistic or unachievable; ultimately, of course, the teacher is the final determiner of what is workable.) Since kindergarteners, first graders, and second graders have shorter attention spans, for them, ten to twenty minutes is more realistic and successful. Holding meetings right before lunch or recess makes it easier to stick to the time limit. Class meetings may dovetail into Social Studies or Health in elementary or middle school. In high school, homeroom seems to be the most natural place.

- **TEACH NON-PUNITIVE PROBLEM-SOLVING SKILLS AND HAVE FAITH IN STUDENT ABILITIES.** Students will have the opportunity to develop competency in cooperation, understanding of self and others, good listening and speaking skills, confidence, and critical thinking. With this in mind, the guiding teacher resists taking over the meeting. Instead, as a facilitator, she asks questions that give students a chance to evaluate the pros and cons of choices. For example, "So you mean, it's okay to beat up Scott?" This type of inquiry helps students discover the fallacy of their thinking and opens the door for queries that lead to win-win solutions, such as, "What do you think will solve this problem?" Students will learn much more from their own suggestions that don't work than from merely following the suggestions of a "boss teacher" (even though your answer may seem to be a better one). Remember, follow-through is always greater when the idea comes from a student's brain, heart, and mouth. Ownership and follow-through go hand in hand. Also, allowing students to solve the same problems repeatedly provides the practice needed to learn the skills. This gives students a chance to gain insights into why similar problems reoccur, evaluate what hasn't worked, and create more effective strategies.

SWW&MIR is the perfect vehicle for teaching conflict resolution and problem-solving skills. Once the students have mastered the five-step process and have embraced the idea that it is the acceptable and successful way to solve problems at school, many issues will be solved on their own. Through this process, children learn to use "I" messages, listen to each other, make eye contact, and acknowledge feelings in individual relationships. These learnings can be carried into group problem-solving.

Utilizing meeting time for students to practice problem-solving skills provides further chances for them to develop competency (as discussed in Chapter 3). Putting problems on the agenda for the class meeting acknowledges their importance while allowing tempers, which tend to flare in the heat of the moment, to subside.

CLASS MEETING GUIDELINES: PART IV

At the first few class meetings, the teacher models being a leader. The leader's job is to maintain safety and keep everyone on topic. The teacher guides the class to establish a safe atmosphere by asking, "What rules will help you feel safe to share your opinions in our meetings?" The following are essential:

- Show respect for everyone's opinion by not using put-downs.
- Listen with eyes on each person speaking.
- Only speak when holding the talking stick or other agreed-upon object.

By the time class meetings are introduced, lessons demonstrating good listening, including eye contact, will have been established. Rules for the talking stick are easy to establish (see detailed explanation of the talking stick in the "Family Meetings" section of this chapter). Charney suggests role-playing and discussing physical put-downs, such as rolling eyes or other facial expressions, as well.

The teacher establishes that the purpose of the meetings is to solve problems as a class, emphasizing that everyone's opinion is important and valuable. The goal is to create win-win solutions. Blaming and shaming do not serve this purpose.

As soon as students are familiar and comfortable with the structure of class meetings, they may be able to take turns with some of the roles. Role responsibility empowers students. With teacher guidance, younger students can:

- Colead the meetings
- Be the assistant secretary, using drawings as well as key phrases to take notes
- Take charge of the peace bell
- Observe the meeting for good listeners

Young leaders may need support from the adult guide—for example, "Mary, remind the class of the talking stick rule" or "You may need to remind the class that we are looking for a win-win solution to what to do about people being left out of games."

People unfamiliar with five- and six-year-olds are often surprised when I suggest that they take notes during meetings or even journal write. However, their drawings or strings of letters are their beginning writings—a skill that should be nurtured as early as possible.

The peace bell (also explained in the "Family Meetings" section of this chapter) is a valuable tool in class meetings. In fact, it is a valuable tool in most areas of life!

The student designated as the observer should be given a minute at the end of the meeting to describe some positive listening habits that he or she noticed. Occasionally, this is a useful teaching tool for someone that has difficulty with listening skills. However, steer away from choosing only poor listeners to man this post; this will not empower students. From fourth grade on up, students are eventually able to step into all of these roles. Another practical position is that of timekeeper. This individual times brainstorming sessions, makes certain the meeting ends on time, and monitors any other part of the meeting with a time limit.

Problem-solving is one of the main purposes of class meetings. For the first meeting, the main goal is to model how the process works and to reinforce the adult's faith in the students' abilities to solve problems. Therefore, a simple problem—a messy classroom, for example—would be a wise choice.

Begin with brainstorming (see Chapter 9 if you need a refresher). This is one time when the talking stick is set aside. Remind the students to have fun with this and come up with as many suggestions as possible in the three or so minutes allotted. Start the timer and start writing every idea suggested, verbatim, on the board, computer, or chart paper. Some student suggestions might be:

1. "A daily Clean Class Monitor to throw away any papers on the floor or out of place."

2. "And a second monitor to store, for ten days, reusable supplies, books, and jackets that are out of place."

3. "The daily Clean Class Monitor should write the names on the board of people that are not doing their share."

4. "Allow one-minute clean-up time before each recess and before going home."

5. "Individual waste baskets at each team group of desks."

6. "Anybody caught not cleaning up their mess has to stay in at recess and clean the whole classroom."

7. "A daily inspector to dismiss clean team groups for each recess and for going home."

When the timer goes off, it's time to discuss the *pros and cons* of the ideas suggested. For the first few meetings, the teacher/leader may need to remind students again, "We are looking for a win-win solution to the problem. Learning from our mistakes is a positive outcome. Our focus needs to be on growth, not blame. Cooperation and compromise lead to growth." (You'll notice that suggestions number 3 and 6 are more punitive than productive. Students that are used to being punished may have the greatest difficulty thinking in terms of win-win solutions. In the long run, their growth and cooperation may be the most noticeable and satisfying for all concerned.)

Some additional helpful guidance tasks:

- Remind the group of their rules for creating a safe space for everyone to state their opinions.
- Draw attention to the poster of "Three R's and an H for Focusing on Solutions: Related, Respectful, Reasonable, Helpful."
- Make certain the talking stick starts and ends in the same place in the circle to maintain the equal importance of each individual's voice.

- Use the timer in order to stick to the agreed-upon time limit for the meeting. Also, the timer is useful if some students go on and on.

As the talking stick goes around the circle, other ideas might stem from the original ones suggested. Sometimes the talking stick needs to go around twice, as one person's comment may stimulate another thought or idea.

If the solution is for a problem that concerns the majority of the class, a majority vote is appropriate. The majority rules, unless there is strong dissension. If that's the case, the issue may need to be tabled and put on the agenda for the next meeting. This is partly because dissenting people may sabotage the solution. However, even if they do not, this defeats the purpose of unifying the class and valuing all opinions.

If the class generally agrees, the leader ends the problem-solving portion of the meeting with a summary of the class decision—e.g., "For one week we will try allowing one minute clean-up time before each recess and going home. Also, we've decided to take turns being daily inspector to dismiss clean team groups for each recess and going home. Next meeting we'll evaluate to see if it is working or if we need to put it back on the agenda."

This is the perfect segue for introducing the agenda in the first meeting. You could say something like, "At each meeting we will have an agenda of problems to be solved. Any of us may put problems to be solved on the agenda. It may be problems involving the whole class, or it may be a problem between two people. Before a problem between two or three individuals can be put on the agenda to be brought to the meeting, all the parties involved must agree to involve the class in possible solutions."

Some ideas of places for the agenda to live are on a bulletin board, a box, or a notebook. The person who writes a problem on the agenda should also include the date of their entry. It is wise to only allow students to write on the agenda at the beginning of recess and going-home time; this will help you ensure that class starts on time. Kindergarteners and first graders may dictate their problem, or they may draw and sign it.

Putting items on the agenda allows for a cooling-off period. The advantage of the notebook is that solutions to problems can also be recorded there. Solutions that may or may not have worked in the past can give insight into current problems.

When discussing a problem on the agenda, the writer of the problem will start the talking stick and speak first. Problems on the agenda involving an absent student need to be tabled until that individual is present. As in the five-step process used in individual problem-solving, students are asked to briefly share their problem and feelings in the class meeting. If students give a laundry list of complaints or have trouble being brief, asking, "What are you the most upset about?" assists them in being more succinct and recognizing the heart of the concern. This question is also helpful in creating ease for the overwhelmed child. If there are just a few people involved, they will have their say next. If there are more than a few, the talking stick will just move to each individual in the circle in turn after the writer of the problem has had their say. Once the talking stick has gone all the way around the circle, it's time to brainstorm for solutions.

After brainstorming is the time for the talking stick to make the rounds once again. This time, everyone can have their say about the pros and cons of the possible solutions brainstormed. The students involved in the problem choose the solution that seems to be most helpful. If they don't agree, they pick a private time in the next twenty-four hours to come up with a solution that works for both or all concerned. Depending on the degree of their disagreement, their discussion may need to take place in the teacher's field of vision or hearing. Their agreement needs to show mutual respect. Also, they need to state when in the following thirty-six hours their solution will take effect. This supports and assists them in being accountable and keeping their commitment.

At the end of the meeting, do a debrief: have participants share their thoughts and feelings about that day's meeting. Ask for volunteers to share with the group any insights gained or decisions reached. Make certain that the class is clear about the agreed-upon solution.

Decisions reached, solutions to problems, and items needing further discussion should be documented in a class meeting journal as a meeting comes to a close. Teachers and students can include their thoughts and insights gained from the meeting in the journal. Students that are just beginning to learn to write can illustrate their thoughts there after the meeting. Until an observer of positive listening skills is chosen, this is an appropriate time for the leader to give recognition to the class for their listening, problem-solving, and other skills noticed.

Finally, it's helpful to end with a fun activity, if time allows, in order to further enhance a sense of community. This is especially true if the problem-solving session has been intense. One way to release tension and acknowledge individuals is with a game called, "You are really good at _____ guessing game." In this game, either the teacher or the students write one sentence about each student in the class, describing something that individual is good at or does well. The teacher reads the sentence in question form—for example, "Who is good at drawing?"; "Who listens to you when you are talking?"; or "Who is a good handball player?" If the wrong name is guessed, more than one ego is boosted. This activity need only take a few minutes of class meetings, as long as every class member is acknowledged throughout the weeks to come.

Classroom meetings take some time and organizing, but the benefits outweigh the time invested. Classes with behavior problems will find the meetings a timesaver in the long run. As Sura Hart and Victoria Kindle Hodson write in their book *The Compassionate Classroom,* "When students are involved in making decisions about classroom life, they feel engaged, interested, empowered, and hopeful. The more decisions students make, the more this is so, since many needs are met for them: participations, inclusion, respect, consideration, trust, power over their environment and their learning."

PART II

FOUNDATION BUILDING

CHAPTER 11:

FRAMEWORK ACTIVITIES

The purpose of these activities is to provide the framework to increase children's mastery of the SWW&MIR five-step process, both at home and in school. These exercises provide a foundation for the understanding of the "Formal Introduction Lesson" located in Appendix A of this book.

PROCEDURE

The lessons are progressive. As the parent or teacher, you decide within which level the majority of your children are functioning. However, understanding the adult's role is crucial to every level. The tenets of the adult's role support all of the lessons.

As you introduce SWW&MIR's five-step process, either incidentally or formally, you will probably find it necessary and beneficial to reinforce the process through visiting the "Feelings Lessons" that follow.

Use these lessons during story time, in association with the story of the day. Parents can incorporate these lessons into bedtime stories. Every good story has a problem that elicits feelings. Also, use these lessons incidentally, as the occasion merits. All it takes to stop the perfect lesson plan or the family trip to Grandma's is one unhappy child. This is when I take a few minutes and use the upset to assist the individuals involved in dealing with their feelings and needs. It dissipates the discordant atmosphere and creates a more receptive, cooperative one. In the long run, it saves time and everyone's peace of mind.

FUNDAMENTAL CONCEPTS

- Knowing that feelings are not bad, good, right, or wrong makes it safer to get in touch with and deal with them.
- Recognizing and talking about feelings brings about safer, more satisfying results in relationships with others.
- Realizing and understanding that different people may feel differently about the same situation paves the way for greater ease in communication and problem-solving.

RECOGNITION OF FEELINGS IN SELF AND OTHERS

The adult's role is the foundation. Your job is to:

- Listen to and give empathetic feedback about an individual's feelings. This demonstrates respect and often dissipates the feeling. ("Are you angry?")
- Assist children in identifying their feelings and acknowledging feelings without judgment in order to build a sense of trust and safety. ("Are you mad because you're having so much fun playing and you don't want to go home right now?") Remember that the feelings are not personally directed at you.
- Ask questions for understanding. This contributes to a problem-solving atmosphere. Telling children what they "should" have done or blaming individuals does not. ("What happened that's upsetting you?")
- Use "I" messages. This models an excellent communication strategy. It improves understanding and lessens defensiveness. ("I feel sad when I see someone hurt others. I want everyone to feel safe in this family (or class).")
- Involve the class or family in establishing clear limits, responsibilities, expectations, and consequences in order to create ownership, greater follow-through, a sense of security, and empowerment. Class or family meetings are important mediums for preventing and solving most problems.

- Encourage responsibility and independence. These qualities build self-esteem and lead to self-discipline.

Model all of the above. Modeling is one of the best teaching tools. Children are great mimickers. If I frequently say to children when they fall, "Are you all right?" it isn't long before I hear them saying it themselves when someone falls.

All of these factors contribute to an environment in which it is safe to recognize and state feelings, which leads to solving problems instead of blaming or punishing. Because of this, independent thinking, learning, growth, and cooperation are more likely to thrive.

BEGINNING-LEVEL ACTIVITIES FOR YOUNG CHILDREN

Language Arts Activities

1. **STORIES** provide unlimited opportunities to develop an understanding of feelings.

   - Children predict what the story may be by studying the illustrations. Possible discussion questions: "What do you think is happening in the story? What might the people be feeling? How can you tell?"
   - Stop a few times during and after a story to *explore strong feelings* of anger, sadness, fear, or happiness

that might be present: "How might individuals be feeling? What might be causing them to feel that way? How can you tell?"

2. **JOURNAL WRITING** is an excellent follow-up for the majority of activities and lessons in this book. When young children are at the pre-writing level, their drawings are their writing.

Games

1. **VOCABULARY GAMES.** Too often we adults assume children are defying us when they simply are not fully understanding some of our words. The understanding of the following words in young children increases their ability to solve problems and communicate: "Before/After;" "Sad/Mad/Glad;" "Is/Is Not;" "Same/Not the Same;" "Same/Different;" "Fair/Not Fair." In her book *Raising a Thinking Child*, Myrna Shure suggests that when these words are introduced in game form, children associate them with fun. Because of this, they will be more likely to make this vocabulary their own and consequently use it when they are involved in actual problem solving. An example of a game with words is, "Today we're going to play with the words 'Is' and 'Is Not.' I'll go first. A shoe *is to wear on my foot. It is not* to wear on my ear. Right or wrong? Who has another 'Is/Is Not' pair?" In the classroom, follow up on this by including these word pairs in the way you usually introduce vocabulary—word of the day, word buttons, word wall, writing/spelling lessons, etc.

2. **LISTENING GAME.** Start by telling the children, "We are going to play a game called 'Using Your Ears.' You won't be able to see my face. Your ears will help you figure out what I am feeling." Go behind a screen or cover your face. "Raise your hand if you can tell what I am feeling." Cry, laugh, scream, growl, whine, or grumble. When the correct response is given, elicit what clues helped to solve the puzzle. Elaborate on how ears can help to tell us how someone is feeling. Repeat with some of the other sounds. Some of the children may want to try being the ones to make the sounds as well.

3. **OBSERVATION GAME.** The name of this game is "Using Your Eyes," but don't tell the children this before you start. Instead, tell them, "When I say, 'Action!' raise your hand if you can tell what I'm feeling." Pantomime sadness, happiness, fear, or anger, then say, "Action!" When the correct response is given, elicit what clues helped to solve the puzzle. Help the children elaborate on how eyes help us to understand how someone else is feeling. Repeat with one or two more feelings. The players will probably want to pantomime some of the feelings. A fun ending for this game is to lead the group in a Silent Cheer. Use the motions of a cheer: hands raised above your head and a wide-open mouth. This is a useful tool any time for totally active yet silent participation.

ADVANCED-LEVEL ACTIVITIES FOR CHILDREN
Language Arts

1. As a class or family, **DISCUSS** times when individuals recall being sad, mad, happy, or afraid. Use a story, poem, chant, song, etc. to stimulate memories.

2. Invite everyone to contribute illustrations to a **FAMILY OR CLASS CHART** about each feeling. (See Appendix B for examples of children's drawings.)

3. Write and illustrate a **CLASS OR FAMILY BOOK** for each feeling. For example: "I felt happy when . . ."; "I was sad when . . ."; etc.

4. Children act out or use puppets to **DRAMATIZE** stories involving the basic feelings. Discuss the feelings afterward. Possible discussion questions: "Was anybody feeling mad in the story?"; "What may have caused him/her to feel mad?" Do the same with happy, sad, and afraid.

"Feeling Detective"
(Feeling Card Recognition Game)
This activity graphically illustrates that different people may feel differently about the same situation while also assisting children and adults in recognizing their own feelings.

Materials needed: Three "Feeling Response Cards" for every single person (see Appendix B).

Directions: The "Feeling Detective" game will go more smoothly if the adult reads the Helpful Hints below before introducing the game. To create greater individual involvement, elicit situations from the family or class that cause them irritation, frustration, anger, sadness, etc., or use some of the "Situations" in Appendix B that are common concerns of many elementary school children.

Helpful Hints:

1. You will probably need to remind the participants, "There are no right or wrong answers. What makes you mad may make someone else sad." In addition, when one person holds up a sad card while everyone else is holding up a mad card, commend the person. Say briefly that this is what being a "Feeling Detective" is all about, listening more to our own heart and brain rather than paying attention to what cards other people are holding up. This reinforces your message that feelings may vary from individual to individual, from situation to situation, and encourages others to have the courage to acknowledge their feelings.

2. If an individual holds up the yellow card (happiness), it is usually because she/he is

uncomfortable with feelings. Without drawing attention to the person, this is a perfect time to remind everyone, "Identifying your feelings takes courage, concentration, and practice at first. It's not always easy, but I think you'll find the payoff worth it." Many young children are quicker to identify their feelings than many adults are because they have not had as much practice denying or ignoring them. As the one who is uncomfortable with this subject grows in confidence and trust and begins to feel safer within the group, his comfort with this subject will increase.

3. If a player holds up the happy card when the group is asked to show how they feel about name-calling, restate the situation: "Think about the name you HATE to be called." This frequently brings a sad or mad card response.

4. When someone responds with "This is dumb!" it is often because the person could be feeling vulnerable, apprehensive, inadequate, overwhelmed, or probably even a little bit dumb. This may be the perfect opportunity to discuss how feelings can make any of us feel "dumb," "out of control," "weak," "small," "out of it," "embarrassed," or even "less than."

Introduction: "I am going to say some things that might make you mad or sad. When I say something that makes you mad, hold up the card you will show me. Yes, the pink card is the mad card." Repeat with happy and sad cards. You will need to remind everyone of the purpose of the game: "This game will help you identify your feelings about different situations. It will show you that people may have different feelings about the exact same situation. There are no right or wrong answers."

"Who can tell me what a detective is?" (Answer: "A person who searches for and finds the truth.") "What do you think a Feeling Detective does?" (Answer: "Identifies feelings.") "How many of you think you are good Feeling Detectives for yourself? Feelings can be uncomfortable." Illustrate with an appropriate strong feeling of your own. For instance, I personally hate to be put down in front of others. It makes me feel embarrassed and ashamed or worthless. After you've given your example, tell the children, "It takes a lot of courage and honesty to say your feelings. As a 'Feeling Detective' you may learn some new ideas about yourself. I think we are ready."

Playing the Game: "With your cards, show how you feel when . . ." State some of the situations that you previously elicited from the group:

- "You are blamed for something you didn't do."
- "Someone cheats when playing a game with you."
- "Someone changing the channel on TV right when you're in the middle of watching a program."

As sad or mad cards are held up for the exact same situation, point that out with, "Look around. Notice how each one of us may feel differently about an identical situation. Remember, feelings aren't right or wrong. They just are." Continue with a few more situations to further illustrate that statement.

- "How do you feel about being bossed around?"
- "How do you feel when someone is mimicking your friends and you?"

Closure: Make certain the last statement is a positive one. For example, "How does it make you feel when someone says what a great job you did?" When they display the happy cards, respond with, "And you did do a great job!"

This may be a good time to follow with journal writing, introduced with, "Think about what you learned about feelings today . . . Did you have any surprises?" After journal writing, the children may want to partner share and/or share with the group. End with a reminder about confidentiality and a brief discussion about what they think the object of the game was. The emphasis should not be on "right or wrong" answers. The purpose of this discussion is twofold:

1. For the leader to assess what the players learned and how they are feeling.

2. For the players to gain reinforcement of what they have learned.

Games

1. "ACT OUT THE FEELING"

This game is designed to increase children's empathy and understanding of nonverbal clues.

Materials: Chart paper and "Some Common Situations that Cause Upsets" (Appendix B) or pictures of pleasurable and mildly upsetting situations.

Introduction: "We are going to act out some feelings. First we need to talk about how people may act, what they may do, and what they may look like when they are feeling a certain way." Guide the players by discussing and charting as a group the physical responses for the emotions they will be acting out. For example, "angry" looks like clenching fists, stomping feet, scowling faces, etc.

Directions: "Find your own body space. You will be using your whole body to act out how you feel in each of the situations I describe and/or in the pictures I show you. You will need a space of your own, because this game will be more fun if everyone is safe."

Activity: "First I will demonstrate." After you demonstrate, everyone tries to guess what feeling was being acted out. "Now it's your turn." The leader calls out a situation or shows pictures. The participants act out the feelings they might have in that situation, or they pair up and take turns acting and guessing what the other is feeling. In either case, be sure to end with a few happy situations (for example: finding a kitten).

Closure: Guide the group in reflecting on, "What did you notice? What did you learn? What was your favorite part? Anything you didn't like? How are you feeling now?" Make certain all are "feelin' fine" at the end.

2. "USING YOUR EARS" ADVANCED VERSION

This game is meant to develop children's concept that tone of voice and inflection can indicate how another is feeling.

Materials: The three "Feeling Response Cards" (see Appendix B) for every person, or writing materials—for example, individual whiteboards and pens. You may need to use a screen or sheet of paper to hide your facial expressions.

Introduction: "One way of noticing how others are feeling is listening to their voice. Who thinks they have excellent ears for hearing how people are feeling?"

Activity Directions: "I am going to change my voice to indicate the three basic feelings. Your challenge is to identify the feeling and write it on your whiteboard or hold up a 'Feeling Response Card' that indicates the feeling you heard." Change your tone of voice and intonation to indicate the three basic feelings, varying the order of feelings with each of the following (and/or similar) statements:

- "It's my birthday."
- "My sister is coming with us."
- "He called me 'the boss.'"
- "They took my drawing."
- "I'm on the blue team."

Example: "I'm in the outfield," said like you're mad balls never come your way, or said as if you're sad because you're a better first baseman, or said like you're proud and excited because yesterday you caught a fly ball. (With the next statement, vary the order of feelings.)

The leader may need to do some feelings more than once. If the players are not sure of the feeling after two tries, this is an excellent opportunity to remind them, "When you are not certain how someone is feeling, it is a good idea to ask, 'How are you feeling?'"

Closure: Guide the group in reflection by asking, "What did you notice? What did you learn? Can you think of a time when someone said they were fine, but their voice did not sound like they were fine? Is hearing how people are feeling hard or easy to do? Keep practicing on your own. We can play this game again."

Activities for All Levels

1. CIRCLE TALK

This activity is useful in family meetings when one or two kids are especially upset, and in the classroom when one or more students do not seem ready to learn because of upsets they have carried into class. This activity creates understanding, empathy, and bonding in most any group. With a class, it has the added benefit of raising the level of children's readiness to learn.

Materials: No materials are necessary. However, an item such as a smooth stone, something heart-shaped, or a stuffed animal, etc., can be passed to denote the speaker and serve as a reminder that, "Only one person speaks at a time."

Directions:
   a) When the occasion merits, allow about fifteen minutes (depending on the size of the group) to go around the circle for all to say their feelings and why, *if* they want to do so. For example:
      • "I'm feeling sad because my hamster died."
      • "I'm happy and excited because my birthday is Thursday!"

   b) Each person has the right to pass.

   c) The ideal setting is a circle, because it allows everyone to have eye contact and adds to the sense of inclusion.

Introduction: Explain the activity and models with an "I am feeling . . ." statement. For example:

   • "I am feeling sad because I see a lot of people forgetting to be kind to each other."

- "I am feeling happy because everyone in our class is here today."

Before passing the turn to the first person that is ready, state the rules: "Every person will have a turn. If you do not want to say what you're feeling, just say, 'Pass,' and pass the object on to your neighbor. When it is not your turn, your eyes and ears need to be on the speaker."

Activity: Participants take turns saying their feelings and why, if they know, or saying, "Pass," if they do not wish to speak.

If they say their feelings but are uncertain about why they're experiencing them, the leader might help the speaker's understanding by asking, "What are you thinking about?"

If two individuals are upset with each other, they may want to use this time to "Say What's Wrong and Make It Right" or set up a time for doing so.

If someone is upset with another who is not present, it is better if she/he doesn't use their name, as that person isn't there to tell their side.

This is not a time for advice giving. It is more of a time for acknowledging feelings and clearing the air.

Closure: "Let's take a deep breath. How is everybody feeling?" If there are a few who appear upset, they may need some private time to write in their journal or pursue some other techniques (see Chapter 8).

2. THE NEVER-ENDING LESSON

This is one of the most important tools/lessons of all. It does not include a formal introduction. No materials are needed. It is an excellent way to introduce "Say What's Wrong and Make It Right," incidentally and to individuals. It involves the children in active participation and closure. Also, it is great modeling and reinforcement once the process has been introduced.

When problems arise naturally during the day, guide individuals through all of the five-step process, making certain to include step 3. For example, "Michael, tell Johnny how you feel about him pushing your books on the floor"; "Johnny, tell Michael what made you feel like pushing Michael's books on the floor." A conversation that could arise from this situation might look like this:

JOHNNY: "I'm mad because you wouldn't play basketball with me."

MICHAEL: "We always play basketball, and you always win. You hog the ball, and I don't get a chance to improve my game."

JOHNNY: "How about if I become your trainer, and we just spend the next few weeks improving your game?"

MICHAEL: "Okay, but if you call me names or make fun of me, I'm through with you and basketball."

JOHNNY: "I promise it'll be fun. This how my dad helped me improve my game."

ADULT: "How are you both feeling now?"

JOHNNY: "Kinda excited. I think this will be fun."

MICHAEL: "I'm not sure. I'll let you know in a few days. It'll depend on what kind of a trainer he is."

ADULT: "I'm writing myself a note to remember to check with you two on Friday."

CHAPTER 12:

TARGET LESSONS FOR HOME AND SCHOOL

The purpose of these lessons is to support and reinforce the lessons in this book, including the Framework Activities from Chapter 11, the incidental teaching of SWW&MIR's five-step process, and "The Formal Introduction of the Five-Step Process."

LEARNING TO USE "I" MESSAGES

The Formula

I feel_______when______________. I want/would like______________.
(the upset) *(the solution)*

Example: "I **feel** irritated **when** you borrow my scissors and don't return them. **I would like** for you to put them back in their place so I don't have to go searching for scissors when I'm ready to use them."

Key Ingredients

1. Look in the other person's eyes.
2. Use an assertive (not aggressive or whiny) tone of voice.
3. Focus on solution rather than blame.
4. Ask "What?" instead of "Why?" questions.

Reinforcing "I" Messages

1. **CREATE A FAMILY OR CLASS "*I WANT . . .*" CHART OR BOOK.** Create a chart or book as a group about what makes each individual feel better when they are upset. Some people prefer the phrase, "I would like . . ." or "I prefer . . ." Use a book or story about feelings to stimulate their thinking. Then discuss: "What are some ways to make you feel better when you are upset?" Accept most answers. However, steer away from inappropriate responses, such as money, candy, kisses at school, eating dirt, etc. Follow this with, "What will solve the problem?" Use the children's illustrations and words to make the book or chart.

2. **ROLE-WORKING:** Practice the use of "I" messages through role-working, using family or class books about feelings or situations of upsets from stories.

Directions: "You have learned that you have the right and responsibility, when you have a problem with someone, to tell the person, to 'Say What's Wrong and Make It Right.' *Today we are going to practice giving* 'I' messages." Model an "I" message about an upset. For example, "I feel frustrated when people make a mess and leave it for me to clean up. I would prefer that people clean up after themselves. Now I would like to hear some 'I' messages from you." Some examples might be:

- "I feel sad and angry that you took my new blouse without asking. I would like for you to check with me if you want to borrow something of mine." (At school a child might have a similar "I" message about another student taking something from their desk without asking.)
- "I'm mad because you told me you'd practice baseball with me yesterday, but you went off with your friends instead. When we make a plan, I want us to stick with the plan or at least talk about it before changing it."

After each "I" message, ask the group to think about how they feel hearing those requests. After five or six people have had a turn stating an "I" message, debrief with a discussion about how the various requests affected each one of them. If there's time, role-working an incident or two with the Key Ingredients in mind (refer to earlier in this chapter) will reinforce this important skill.

At school, after several people have had a turn, a

different way of debriefing is to close with a few class choral-echo responses of an "I" message. Primary age children enjoy choral readings. For example, a child volunteers, "I feel sad if someone won't get off the swing when it's my turn. I want people to take turns." The group choral-echoes the child's exact "I" message in the three parts. For example:

CHILD: "I feel sad . . ."

GROUP ECHO: "I feel sad . . ."

CHILD: ". . . if someone won't get off the swing when it's my turn."

GROUP ECHO: ". . . if someone won't get off the swing when it's my turn."

CHILD: "I want people to take turns."

GROUP ECHO: "I want people to take turns."

Fourth graders, fifth graders, and older students are enthusiastic about role-working. For debriefing, involving them in acting out a few "I" message situations will increase their understanding and appreciation of the results.

3. **RECOGNITION AND MODELING**: Encourage individuals when they remember to use an "I" message by showing appreciation. This is important during the lesson, but even more meaningful in everyday life. For example,

"You really have the 'I' message down pat, Mary. Great job." This identifies the skill the adult is desirous of teaching. As always, the more often the adults remember to model the use of "I" messages in daily interactions, the quicker this communication skill will become a part of the children's vocabulary.

Adult's Role

1. MODEL THE USE OF "I" MESSAGES WHEN UPSET.

Example: "I feel mad when two or more people gang up on one person. If you have a problem with someone, I would like you to solve it one to one using your words. I would be happy to mediate and support you both."

2. TEACH "SAY WHAT'S WRONG AND MAKE IT RIGHT":
    a) Formally
    b) Informally, as incidents occur

3. REINFORCE THE USE OF KEY INGREDIENTS as listed in Chapter 2.

REINFORCEMENT OF RIGHTS AND RESPONSIBILITIES R&R IN PROBLEM-SOLVING

Acknowledgment
When the children begin to practice these five R&R's, bring recognition to this behavior. For example, you could say, "I love hearing people saying, 'Stop!' when they are upset by

what someone is doing," or "Mark, you are doing a great job of looking in Lisa's eyes and listening to her."

Role-working

As needed, review the five R&R's through role-working of problem-solving.

The Never-Ending Lesson

Adult-guided problem-solving by the children as the situations actually arise throughout the day, incorporating the five R&R's.

Language Arts

Discussing problems in stories forms a foundation and reinforces understanding as the children grow in their abilities. Ask questions such as, "What's the problem? What might be done to solve this problem? Will everyone be happy and safe then? What could they do that would make everyone happy and safe?"

Adult Responsibilities

As the adult, you need to keep in mind the adult responsibilities of:

1. Never choosing to believe one child over the other.

2. Making certain both children listen to each other, make eye contact, have the opportunity to express their feelings, and feel better at closure.

3. Following through and monitoring. Being careful not to turn the program over to the children before they *know* it. When they have internalized the five-step process, they will start solving problems on their own!

Conclusion:

"SAY WHAT'S WRONG AND MAKE IT RIGHT" IN SUMMARY

The key concepts that will provide the foundation for your children's success with SWW&MIR are:

- Responsibility for solving the problem belongs to the people in conflict, not the facilitator.
- Eye contact is the path to the heart.
- The individuals involved should talk about the problem using "I" messages, as well as listen to each person's feelings and view of the situation. This leads to understanding, dissipation of strong feelings, and joint solutions.
- Understanding is developed through questions beginning with "What?" Questions beginning with "Why?" seem accusatory and undermine the process.

The adult facilitator's role determines the ease and speed with which the children are able to assume ownership of the Five-Step Process. The responsibilities of the adult guide are:

- Modeling the Five-Step Process, using "I" messages, willingness to create win-win solutions, and listening to children's input—all qualities that establish a "power-with" environment.
- Assisting children in identifying while acknowledging feelings without judgment reinforces the fundamental concept that feelings are not bad, good, right, or wrong.
- Following the five-step process consistently. (This contributes to mastery and gives each person fair chances to be heard.)
- Coming back to "What are you feeling?" when the process seems to be a struggle.
- Watching or listening to the children's dialogue of the problem to ensure their physical safety.
- Observing children's verbal and nonverbal clues to determine if either of them are still upset and need to talk some more.
- Remaining a neutral guide. (We as adults jump in far too soon and deny children the chances to develop competency in the language and experience of solving problems.)
- Having faith in children's abilities to solve problems includes being aware that they will learn more from their own solutions that don't

work than from the adult providing them with a solution, even if it's technically a better one.

• Being gentle with one's self. Our modeling of accepting mistakes—children's and our own—as part of the learning, growing process is a huge factor in creating a psychologically safe environment.

The major benefits of teaching SWW&MIR to your children are:

• As they become increasingly familiar with the five-step process and see the results, they will use it on their own, without the need for an adult facilitator.

• Children learn alternatives to bullying, tattling, and the use of physical force.

• Because it is about their personal problems, there is a higher degree of motivation to learn the communication skills involved, especially for children with limited speech and limited English.

• Compromise, cooperation, and growth are the result because the goal is creating win-win solutions as opposed to blaming, shaming, and punishing.

• A few minutes talking over the problem in the early stages of an upset is more beneficial than putting it on a back burner, where it will stew until it boils over. Talking about a small problem in the initial stage is a time-saver and contributes to a more positive environment.

Finally, this program is not written in gold. Take it and adapt it to what works best for you and your situation. When in doubt always come back to what everyone is feeling. Feelings are what problems are about, more than the actual situation.

THE BEAUTY OF SWW&MIR

I'd like to close with two stories that further illustrate the joy and value of teaching SWW&MIR to your children:

Johnny's Challenges

Johnny was a bright, hyperactive child in our kindergarten. Academically, he grasped concepts with ease. Socially, he had difficulty relating to others. His way to invite another boy to play was to punch him. It took several different approaches over the months to develop his understanding of personal body space. Finally, our most effective tool was to have him sit outside the class circle with a class list that he was very capable of reading. His job was to watch for classmates being kind and helpful. At the end of the day he was in charge of publicly acknowledging two or three students he had observed being kind or helpful. He was proud and serious about this job. Gradually, his social skills began improving.

On one particular day, Johnny was right on target. When the clean-up signal was given, he joined in enthusiastically, saying out loud, "I'm cleaning up!"

The work project that day had been difficult and messy. It involved cutting four rectangles out of an 8 ½"x11" piece of paper to make a cage for Samantha Snake. Besides working on the "S" sound, the purpose was to develop eye-hand coordination. For many five-year-olds, this task takes great effort and concentration.

The finished cage looked like this. The shaded-in areas are the part that required cutting out.

Johnny was quickly clearing the left-over scraps from each table when he accidentally grabbed Daniel's cage, wadding it up in the process. Daniel's cutting skills were very immature, but he was so motivated that he had worked long and hard to painstakingly cut the rectangles out to form the snake's cage.

Ordinarily, Daniel was quiet and passive. When he saw what Johnny had done to his cage, however, he was so angry he could hardly talk. I could almost see fire coming out of his eyes.

With some trepidation, I guided the two of them through the five-step process. I felt sad for both of them. When they came to step 4, "Tell the other person what you want them to do," I asked Daniel to tell Johnny what could be done to make him feel better.

Daniel was completely speechless. "I could make you another one," Johnny offered eagerly.

This appeased Daniel somewhat. Off he went to recess. Johnny set about to recreate Daniel's cage. This is especially noteworthy because cutting was as difficult for Johnny as it was for Daniel.

Johnny's reproduction was far from perfect, even though he spent his entire recess on the endeavor.

When he presented his offering, though, Daniel thanked him sincerely, and seemed happier. What could have been a disaster had turned into a win-win for both. Daniel was comforted. Johnny felt good about himself for making things right rather than guilty for what he had done by accident. To this day, I am grateful to have been witness to this heart-to-heart solution.

Building Lifetime Skills

LeeAnn, a coworker, observed SWW&MIR in action when Deedee Carr and I facilitated our kindergarteners solving conflicts. Also, she was pleasantly surprised to see children on the playground settling problems on their own. After about a month of observation, she was so amazed at the results that she decided to try the five-step process with her own children at home. Her husband's response was, "This will never work."

At first seven-year-old Debbie and four-year-old Brian hated it because the work and responsibility was upon them for solving their disagreements. They were used to their mother doing the work for them. But LeeAnn did not give in.

For about six months she consistently facilitated her two children's resolution of their disputes using the

Five-Step Process. One evening while doing dishes she overheard Brian saying to his older sister, "We need to talk." She held her breath and listened.

To her amazement, the two shared their feelings about Debbie's use and care of Brian's Game Boy. They listened to each other and came up with a plan that pleased both of them. When LeeAnn heard them laughing, she knew she was out of the middle. She was ecstatic! Not only for this moment in time, but she had imparted to them valuable lifetime communication skills.

I leave you with the two preceding stories in hopes that you'll be inspired to adopt "Say What's Wrong and Make It Right" into your family and professional communication.

Every time I have considered giving up on the completion of this book, a parent, teacher, counselor, principal, aide, grandparent, or an ex-student has told me how SWW&MIR is still making a difference in their lives. And then I recall the children I've seen blossom as a result of solving their own problems and connecting with their fellow human beings.

The other impetus for going forward with this book has been when I've overheard an adult telling two children who are in conflict, "Shake hands and be friends," without investigating their feelings, the root of their disagreement, or what a win-win solution for the two of them might be. From experience, I know the two will be back in the fray in the next day or two, if not in the next few hours. I am especially sad because the perfect opportunity for peace, growth, and a realistic, happy ending have been completely circumvented.

If learning the entire five-step process seems overwhelming, just start with minor issues or trying a small piece of it:

- Using "I" messages when you are upset.
- Asking others when they are upset, "What are you feeling?"
- Making eye contact while communicating with another.
- Asking, "What can we do to make things right?"

"Say What's Wrong and Make It Right" is not a simplistic fix for the moment; rather, it's a proven technique that reveals the root of the problem and finds a solution. This process develops responsibility, assertive communication, and problem-solving skills that continue to serve and grow with the individual.

On a personal note: I can attest to the endorphin rush that accompanies this process. I feel it whether I am a participant in the conflict-resolution process or an observer. Many times when I'm leading two combatants through the five steps, there is an observable turning point where they sincerely connect. I can see it on their faces and hear it in their caring solutions. Witnessing the harmony generated by these two people who were so upset with each other a short time ago always warms my heart.

As time goes by, what's equally gratifying is coming upon a situation that only *appears* to need my assistance. When I ask, "Is there a need to 'Say What's Wrong and Make It Right'?" their proud response of, "No, we already solved it," definitely makes my day!

APPENDICES

APPENDIX A:

⊹————————⊰

CLASSROOM LESSON PLANS

The following lesson plans may be used in an individual classroom. The Active Listening for Feelings lesson is suitable as preparation for the Formal Introduction of the Five-Step Process. Also, it would be an appropriate follow-up lesson to remind students of the value of understanding feelings and the importance of listening to each other.

When time is an issue, as is often the case, a short classroom discussion about situations that cause upsets among the students lays the foundation for the grade-level presentations of the Formal Introduction. This would be most beneficial a day or two before the actual assemblies. At the kindergarten, first, and second-grade level, twenty-five to thirty minutes is the best time allotment. Third through sixth graders will benefit from a thirty- to forty-five-minute interactive lesson. Journal writing is a suggested follow-up for reinforcement and to alleviate strong feelings that may be stimulated by the issues presented.

The Formal Introduction of the Five-Step Process may be used in an individual classroom. However, the greatest impact I've seen on a total school environment has occurred in schools where children in every grade level, as well as the adult personnel, have received the Formal Introduction. When everybody is familiar with "Say What's Wrong and Make It Right" and knows that this is going to be the accepted way of handling disagreements throughout the school, it creates a climate that supports communication, cooperation, and growth.

ACTIVE LISTENING FOR FEELINGS

A. Purpose:

1. To increase individuals' abilities to listen to each other's feelings when solving problems.

2. For individuals to experience how it feels to be listened to and how it feels to not be listened to.

B. Objective:

Each person will be listening to a partner and repeat back the partner's words with accuracy.

C. Materials

1. A story involving a variety of feelings, such as sadness, fear, anger, and happiness. (For example,

Today I Feel Silly & Other MOODS That Make My Day, by Jamie Lee Curtis.)

2. A timer.

3. Handouts of the Six Active Listening Rules (see Appendix B).

D. Introduction:

Read the book, periodically stopping to discuss with the children instances when they may have felt the same way. After three or four discussions, present the challenge, "How many of you think you can be a good listener? This activity will help all of us become even better at listening to others' feelings."

E. Modeling and Input:

1. With a volunteer, do a short demonstration (about forty to sixty seconds each) on active listening of a happy time using the Six Active Listening Rules:

   - Maintain eye contact.
   - Listen! Do not talk.
   - Listen! Do not judge.
   - Listen! Do not offer advice or solutions.
   - Listen to repeat back!
   - *Only* ask questions to understand!

2. Review the Six Active Listening Rules, soliciting from the children if and how the rules were

followed. It's important to emphasize two particular rules, "Listen to repeat back!" and "Do not offer advice or interrupt."

F. Guided Practice 1:

Introduce the exercise: "Think about one of your happiest times. Turn and face an elbow partner." Take a minute to find a partner for anyone without one. "When I say, 'HAPPY TIMES,' face your partner without touching. The person with the fewest buttons will go first. Tell them about one of your happy times. You will both have a turn. You will each have one minute to talk. The timer will ring when it is time to tell your partner what you heard. Then the person with the most buttons will tell about his or her happiest time."

Check for Understanding: Spot check . . . Call on a few listeners to report what they have heard to the group. Make *certain* they have their partner's permission to share what they heard. Check with their partners for:

1. Accuracy

2. How they felt when . . .
   a) they were listened to
   b) they were not listened to

Total Participation: Have everyone in the group tell their partners what they heard. Have everyone check with their partner to see:

1. Whether or not they listened accurately.

2. How the speaker felt.

3. If they followed the Active Listening Rules.

Note: Depending on time and attention spans, Guided Practices 2 and 3 can be done as follow-up lessons.

G. *Guided Practice 2:*

Choose one of the following prompts (1, 2, or 3):
   1. "Think about a time of SADNESS."
     a) A picnic rained out
     b) A friend moving away
     c) Someone hurting your feelings

   2. "Think about a time of ANGER."
     a) Someone taking or breaking something of yours
     b) Someone being unfair to you
     c) Someone teasing or calling you a name you hate

   3. "Think about being SCARED."
     a) Having a nightmare
     b) Seeing a horror movie
     c) Trying something you have never done before

Tell the group about a personal experience you've had related to the feeling, remind the children of the part in the story that connects to the feeling chosen, and elicit from the children a few additions to the list suggested. After student input, give the children these directions:

1. "Turn and face your partner."

2. "When I say, 'BEGIN', the person with the most pockets will start telling about a time when . . ."

3. "You will have __seconds to talk."

4. "When the timer rings, change speakers."

Repeat Check for Understanding and Total Participation.

H. Guided Practice 3:

Start by telling the group, "This time it will be even more difficult to 'Listen to repeat back!' and to not interrupt, especially to give advice. The person speaking is going to tell your partner some problem that is on your mind this week." The teacher tells of a personal example including feelings about the situation. Encourage them to do the same. Elicit from the children a few examples to add to the following list:

- Something difficult for you to accomplish or finish
- Something difficult to say to someone
- Something difficult to quit doing

After student input, give the children these directions:

1. "Turn and face your partner."

2. "Remember, you are listening to repeat back. Do not give advice or try to solve the problem."

3. "When I say, 'BEGIN,' the person wearing the most red will go first."

4. "You will have __ minutes to talk."

5. "When the timer rings, change speakers."

Repeat Check for Understanding and Total Participation.

I. Closure:

After being listened to and hearing their words repeated back, the children may have insights into how they want to proceed with solving their own problems. This would be a perfect time for journal writing and sharing.

J. Check for Understanding of Active Listening for Feelings:

Ask the children to finish the sentence, "Active Listening for Feelings is . . ." The discussion should include their interpretation of the Active Listening rule, but needs to encourage and acknowledge all answers.

Lesson Plan and Teacher Script for the Formal Introduction of the Five-Step Process for Kindergarten through Sixth Grade Students

A. *Objectives:*

- The students will be able to verbalize the five steps when given visual clues.*
- The students will begin to use the five-step process in personal conflict resolution with others.
- The school personnel will guide students through the five-step process until the individuals have become independent problem-solvers.

B. *Materials:*

- Happy, Mad, and Sad Feeling Response Cards for each student participating in the "Feeling Detective" activity. When presenting this lesson to an individual class, it is preferable for each student to have a set of the three color-coded Feeling Response Cards. However, in an assembly, eight to twelve students (each with the three Response Cards) standing in front of and facing the entire grade level will sufficiently demonstrate the concept that "different people may feel differently about the same situation." (See suggested model for cards in Appendix B.)
- Poster of the Five-Step Process
- Picture Clue Cards for each of the Five Steps (see Appendix B.)

C. Introduction:

The following activities are to prepare the students for the Formal Introduction of the Five-Step Process by increasing understanding of their feelings and the role feelings play in problems.

The Teacher's Script

I want to share a way with you to solve problems that can turn sad or angry times into happier times. This program was created to help students learn to solve problems on their own.

Raise your hand if you have ever had a disagreement with somebody else? . . . A brother or sister? . . . A friend? . . . A classmate or a neighbor? Well, I certainly have.

The *number one secret* about problem-solving is . . . the problem is not about what happened, but how the people are FEELING about the situation.

We are going to play a game entitled "Feeling Detective." (This part of the lesson may be done separately. Refer back to Chapter 11 for the complete lesson plan of "Feeling Detective.")

Pass out the three color-coded Feeling Response Cards to each student participating.

That is why each one of you has three feelings cards.

Who can tell me what a detective is? (Answer: A person who searches for and finds the truth.)

What do you think a Feeling Detective does? (Answer: Identifies feelings.)

How many of you think you are good Feeling Detectives for yourself? Feelings can be uncomfortable.

Illustrate with an appropriate strong feeling of your own.

Often it takes a lot of courage and honesty to say your feelings. As a Feeling Detective, you may learn some new ideas about yourself. I think we are ready. I am going to say some things that might make you feel mad, sad, or happy. When I say something that makes you mad, which card will you show me?

Repeat with happy and sad cards.

I think we are ready. Remember, there are no right or wrong answers. Feelings just are. With your cards, show how you feel when:

- Someone special to you leaves or moves away.
- Someone takes or ruins something that belongs to you.
- Someone hurts you.

Notice that people may have different feelings about the exact same situation. With your cards, show how you feel when:

- You make a mistake.
- Someone calls you a name.
- Someone tells you what a great job you did.

You did do a great job of being feeling detectives! Thank you. Now I have somebody else I need to help me.

Go off stage and come back walking and talking like a robot.

Can you guess what I am? (Answer: A robot.)

Do robots get sad? Or mad? (Answer: No.)

Do robots have feelings? (Answer: No! If someone responds with, "R2D2 has feelings," stay in the robot mode with, "I do not know this R2D2, but it sounds like a movie robot.")

Do you think I have problems with other robots? (Answer: No.)

Do you know why? (Students will usually respond with, "Robots don't have feelings.")

I like the way you think. Thank you and good-bye.

Exit, then re-enter as yourself.

Are you a robot? (Answer: No)

You are correct. Because we all have feelings, there are times when we are going to have problems with others. I'm going to name some ways that people try to solve problems. If you think the way I name works, give it a thumbs-up. If you don't think it solves the problem, give it a thumbs-down. If you think it works *some* of the time, give it thumbs-even, like this . . .

Demonstrate with thumbs horizontal and pointing at each other. Check to see if they understand.

Does *yelling* or *screaming help to solve the problem?*

(For primary schoolers, a demonstration with puppets may be helpful.)

What about pushing, hitting, or hurting each other?

Does name-calling work?

See if you can guess this one.

Set up this scene with another adult ahead of time. The other adult comes on stage and starts to take away your boom box, desk chair, laptop, etc. Approach the other person, overacting passivity.

Could you wait twenty minutes? I was just getting ready to use that.

The other person continues walking away with the object, saying, "I just need it for ten minutes. Then I'll bring it back."

But . . . (*shrug your shoulders*) . . . Oh, never mind.

Do you think the both people are satisfied with the outcome?

How many of you are ready to learn a thumbs-up way of resolving conflicts?

If you are upset with someone, who should you tell?

Often the answers will be: "Your mother," "the teacher," "the principal," "the duty," or even "the police." To each of these, your response should be the same.

There is someone you need to tell before that. The correct answer is: "The person you are upset with." That is *secret number* two in the best way to change a difficult situation. *You have definite rights and responsibilities when you have a problem with someone.*

Point to poster of the Five Steps on display (see Appendix B).

STEP 1: When somebody is doing something to you that you don't like, you have the right and responsibility to say, "I don't like that." It's even more powerful if you say exactly what you don't like. For example, "I don't like it when you kick the ball away from the game when you're out. I want you to stop."

Asking the other person to STOP is **STEP 2**. The order of Steps 1 and 2 is interchangeable. If someone is standing on your foot, you are probably not going to say, "I don't like it when you are standing on my foot. Would you please get off?" You are more likely to say, "Please get off my foot. I don't like it when you stand on my foot." Many problems stop right here, once the other person hears your request. That is also true when you accidentally push or run into someone, if you apologize right away, saying, "I'm so sorry. I didn't mean to do that."

STEP 3 is the most important step of all. This is what we call the *heart of the program* (hold up sad & mad cards). If you say your *feelings* and listen to the other person's feelings, most of the time you'll be able to solve the problem—or at least begin to. Remember, the *number one secret* about problem-solving is, "The problem is not about what happened, but how the people are *feeling* about the situation."

Another key ingredient to connecting with and creating empathy for each other is making eye contact. Looking another person in the eye is the path to the heart.

On **STEP 4** you have the right and responsibility to tell the other person what can be done to make you feel better. If you both have contributed in some way to the problem, you need to work out a solution that makes *both* of you feel better. How can someone make you feel better when they've upset you?

Solicit a few responses from the students of what makes them feel better when they are upset. Appropriate answer examples: "Say they're sorry"; "Say they won't do it again"; "Shake my hand." Inappropriate answers often include something material, such as money or a treat. When those pop up, my response is, "It needs to be something that can be done."

STEP 5 is a time for action. If the other person says or does something to make you feel better, how can you let him know that you feel better or at least hear him?

Possible answers: "Thank you"; "I accept your apology."

If you both are a part of the problem and the solution, you both need to take the action the two of you agreed upon. We need to practice these five steps so you will become the master of this tool. I will need two volunteers to act out the steps. I will coach you.

ROLE-WORKING PRACTICE

TEACHER: "I need a name-caller and someone to Say What's Wrong and Make it Right. The class will help you remember the Five-Steps."

1. Guided Practice 1 (for teacher's eyes only)

The teacher should guide the role-workers when the actors forget the five steps, or students can take turns coaching the two role-workers through the five steps using the Five Steps handout located in Appendix B.

You may be pleasantly surprised to know, these are actual dialogues from student role-working sessions. These scripts are not to follow, but to give the teacher the idea of how the role-working may go.

SAY WHAT'S WRONG AND MAKE IT RIGHT

TEACHER TO NAME-CALLER: Call the other person a name or two.

NAME-CALLER: That was a STUPID thing to do.

RESPONDER: Stop calling me names. I don't like it. *(Steps 1 and 2)*

NAME-CALLER: I said the thing you did was stupid.

RESPONDER: I don't like that either. *(Step 1)*

TEACHER TO RESPONDER: Tell her how that made you feel. Remember to look in her eyes.

RESPONDER: It makes me sad. *(Step 3)*

TEACHER TO NAME-CALLER: Tell her how you are feeling.

NAME-CALLER TO TEACHER: I'm mad.

TEACHER TO NAME-CALLER: Don't tell me. Tell her. Don't forget to look in her eyes.

NAME-CALLER TO RESPONDER: I'm mad because you hurried with your part of the poster and messed up your part of our project. Now I feel like we have to start all over to get a good grade. *(Step 3)*

RESPONDER: You all picked the easiest parts to draw and

gave me last choice. I would have never picked that part to draw. I'll take my time and do it over, but I need somebody to help me with the drawing first. *(Step 4)*

NAME-CALLER: I didn't really think about that. Now I feel bad.

TEACHER TO NAME-CALLER: What do you mean by "bad"? Mad? Sad?

NAME-CALLER: I'm sad and embarrassed because we did do that, but it wasn't on purpose. I'm sorry. I'll help you with the drawing part. *(Step 4)*

RESPONDER: Thank you. How about today after school? *(Step 5)*

NAME-CALLER: Good, that way our project can still be on time.

TEACHER TO BOTH: How are you both feeling?

NAME-CALLER: Good.

RESPONDER: Much better.

2. Guided Practice 2

JOEL: I don't like you calling me Joely. *(Step 1)*

ANDY: I'm sorry. I just thought it was sort of a nickname.

JOEL: I don't like it when I get called names.

TEACHER TO JOEL: How does it make you feel?

JOEL: It makes me mad. *(Step 3)*

ANDY: Please stop being mean to me and bullying me. It makes me angry. *(Steps 1, 2, and 3)* Next time I see someone calling you a name I will help you. *(Step 4)*

TEACHER TO ANDY: How will you help?

ANDY TO TEACHER: By asking them to stop.

TEACHER TO ANDY: Tell Joel. Remember to look in his eyes.

ANDY TO JOEL: I'll ask them to stop, but I don't like it when you call me names either. *(Steps 1 and 4)*

JOEL: Okay, I won't be mean to you if you won't be mean to me.

ANDY: You kind of start it first. Let's just make a deal to be friends now.

JOEL: Uhh.

ANDY: I don't think you're really listening to me. I won't want to be your friend if you really don't stop. *(Steps 1, 2, and 4)*

TEACHER TO JOEL: Do you want to be his friend?

JOEL: Sure! High-five, Super Buddy! (They give each other a high-five.) *(Steps 4 and 5)*

TEACHER: Do you want to thank each other? *(Step 5)*

ANDY: Thank you for listening.

JOEL: Thank you for telling me your story. Now we're all good with it. We're all worked out.

3. *Guided Practice 3*

JOHNNY: I don't want you to gang up on me. *(Step 1)* I feel really mad. What made you do that? *(Step 3)*

TEACHER TO SEAN: What made you feel like doing that?

SEAN: I don't know. Sometimes around people I get crazy and act tough.

JOHNNY: Can you never do that again? *(Steps 2 and 4)*

TEACHER TO JOHNNY: Ask if there is something you can do to help.

SEAN: You can be in my gang.

JOHNNY: No, that's not happening. What else?

SEAN: We could be friends.

TEACHER: What does that look like?

SEAN: I won't gang up on him anymore.

TEACHER TO SEAN: Tell him. Don't tell me.

SEAN: I won't gang up on you anymore. You could play with me sometimes.

JOHNNY: Okay, if you won't gang up on me. *(Step 4)*

SEAN: Okay, let's shake on it. *(Step 5)*

Debriefing

Act out the Five Steps. Start by saying, "I'm going to act out your Five Rights and Responsibilities in Problem Solving. See if you can guess what I'm trying to say without looking at the five steps." Then act them out:

> **STEP 1**: Facial expression for "I don't like . . ." and shaking head "no."
>
> **STEP 2**: Hand thrust forward with a stiff elbow as if to say, "Wait!" or "Stop!"
>
> **STEP 3**: Sad and Mad faces; bending ear forward to hear better; pointing to eyes for eye contact
>
> **STEP 4**: Act out shaking hands and/or "I'm sorry."

STEP 5: Act out "thank you" and give the thumbs-up gesture.

"Tell the person you're sitting by a situation where you can use this to solve a problem. Who would like to share how they can see using this process?"

(Allow time for a few responses.)

"Use it in the next two days and it will belong to you. Start with small problems until you've mastered it. Everybody in the entire school is learning this today. Your teachers and yard duty aides can help you. Give yourselves a thumbs-up. You're outstanding students. I look forward to hearing how well you are putting 'Say What's Wrong and Make It Right' into practice."

Teacher Follow-up

Continue role-working other typical problem situations with different volunteers until the majority of the students seem to have a working knowledge of the five steps. With older students, divide them into groups of three or four. In these groups, they can take turns being the coaches and the students involved in the conflict. Provide each group with a copy of the Five-Step Process and Role-working Evaluation Guide (see Appendix B) sheets.

(A big thank you to Kathy Hoffman, MS and PPS in School Counseling, for creating the Robot and Thumbs-Up parts of this lesson.)

APPENDIX B:

⊹————⊰

SUPPORT MATERIALS

THE "SAY WHAT'S WRONG AND MAKE IT RIGHT" FIVE-STEP PROCESS

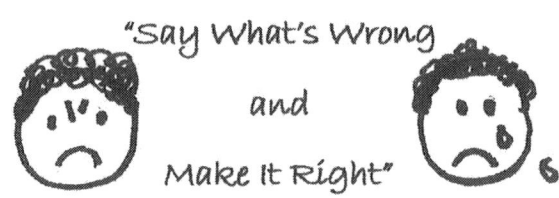

"Say What's Wrong and Make It Right"

Rights and Responsibilities in Communication

1. Tell the other person you don't like what they Are doing.

2. Ask them to STOP.

3. Tell them your feelings about the situation AND listen to their feelings,

4. Tell what you want them to do..

5. Thank them, accept their apology, or Compromise.

Remember: Eye contact Is the path to the Heart!

Karen Taylor-Bleiker/D. Carr

"Say What's Wrong and Make It Right"©

178

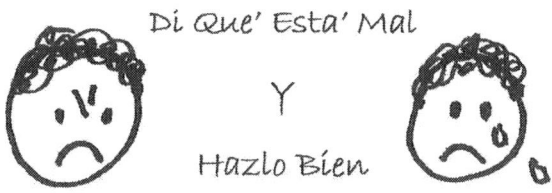

Los derechos y las responsabilidades

en la communicacion:

1. Dile a la otra persona que no te gusta lo que esta' haciendo.
2. Pidele que ya no lo haga.
3. Dile tus sentimientos acerca de la situacion y escucha lo que el o ella te diga de sus sentimientos.
4. Dile lo que quieres que el o ella haga.
5. Agradecele, acepta sus disculpas, o su compromiso.

Recuerda: El contacto visual es el camino hacia el corazon.

Karen Taylor-Bleiker/Deedee Carr

"Say What's Wrong and Make It Right"©

FEELING RESPONSE CARDS FOR THE "FEELING DETECTIVE" GAME

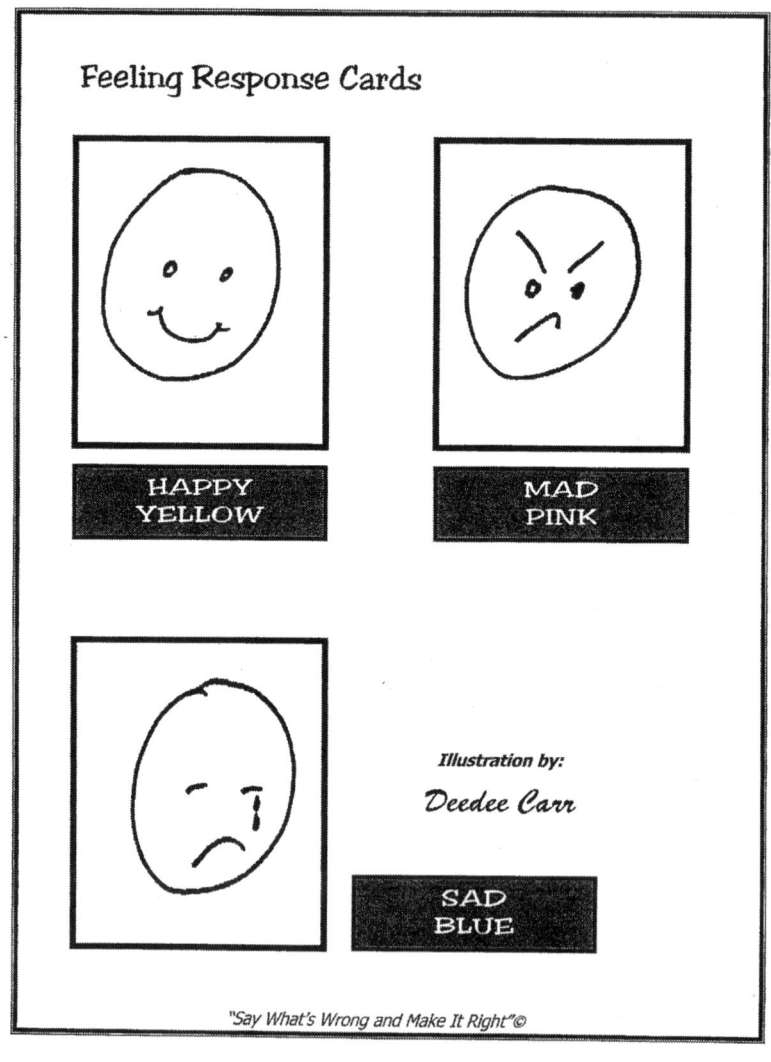

SAMPLES OF CHILDREN'S DRAWINGS
ABOUT FEELINGS

TEACHER: "What are they saying?"

JOHNNY: "I didn't put the words because you can't hear them, but one is being mean."

Do you want me to carry those boxes for you!
Can I help carry those boxes?
Yes!
That would make me feel
moveing
moveing
2-2 B-Ball
Tyler R. Swann
Age 11 1/2

I felt sad when I was told I couldn't play basketball with my friends.

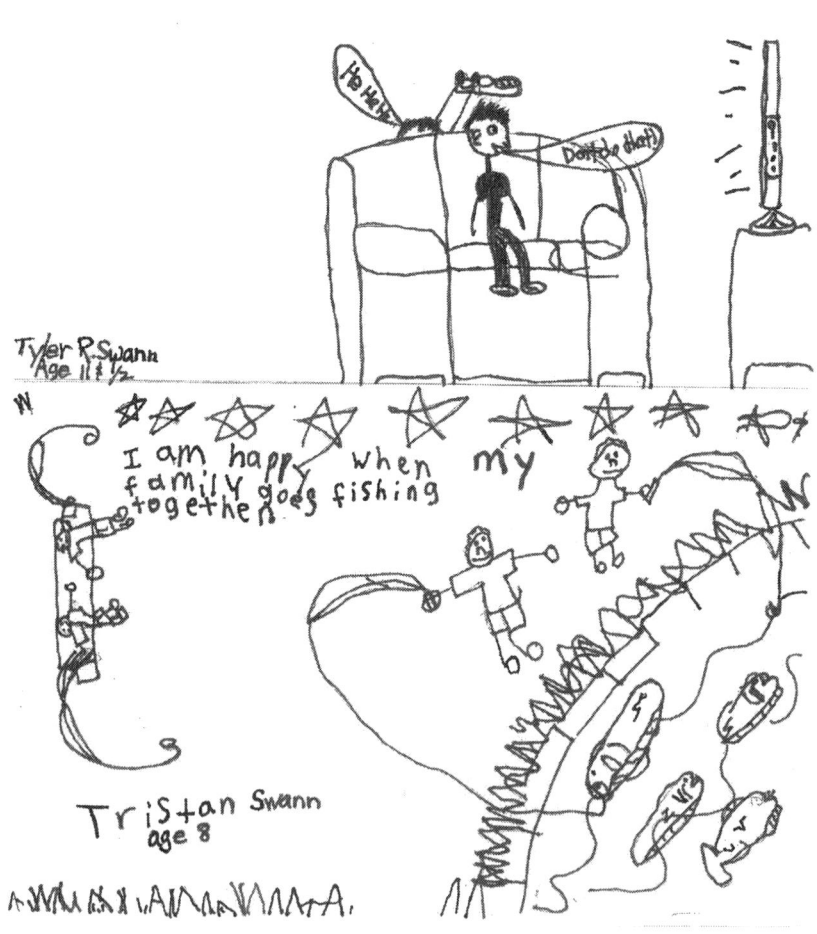

PICTURE CLUE CARDS FOR THE FORMAL INTRODUCTION OF THE FIVE-STEP PROCESS

(drawings by Nathan Savant)

Step 2

Both Speak Their Feelings

Step 3

Listen to Eachother

Step 3

SWW&MIR ROLE-WORKING EVALUATION FORM (FOR 4TH GRADE OR HIGHER)

1. Did both participants:
   - Identify specifically what they were upset about?
   - Speak their feelings?
   - Listen to each other?
   - Use "I" messages?
   - Use eye contact?

2. Did the involved participants create a win-win solution?

3. Did both participants feel fine at closure?

4. Did you have a favorite part?

5. Would you do anything differently?

This is an effective follow-up for reinforcing the key ingredients in the five-step process after role-working. A suggested use would be when individuals are beginning to master SWW&MIR, and then again later on if there are specific areas that need strengthening. It should be used occasionally for review.

LEARNING/TEACHING SEQUENCE OVERVIEW

The Adult Role is the Foundation

Pre-school	*Kindergarten*	*Primary and Upper*
Framework Activities	Framework Activities	Framework Activities
Vocabulary Development Introduce SWW&MIR incidentally as conflicts arise	Vocabulary Development Introduce SWW&MIR incidentally as conflicts arise	Vocabulary Development Introducing SWW&MIR incidentally may be done concurrently with Formal Introduction of SWW&MIR
Continue reinforcing Framework Activities Vocabulary Development Use of SWW&MIR in Conflict Resolution	Formal Introduction of SWW&MIR Target Lessons Reinforcement	Formal Introduction of SWW&MIR Target Lessons Reinforcement

See Learning/Teaching Sequence Outline (Appendix B, pages B193-195) for specific page numbers.

LEARNING/TEACHING SEQUENCE OUTLINE OF "SAY WHAT'S WRONG AND MAKE IT RIGHT"

Preschool

I.   The adult's role is the crucial foundation and remains basically the same throughout all age levels (Chapter 7, pages 45-52 and pages 119-122).

II.   Develop individual's understanding of feelings through Framework Activities (pages 122-124and pages 133-136).

III.   Develop vocabulary understanding relating to feelings and problem-solving (page 123).

IV.   Introduce the Five-Step Process of "Say What's Wrong and Make It Right" incidentally as conflicts arise. (See pages135-136 for "The Never Ending Lesson," a detailed description of *Introducing the Process Incidentally.*)

V.   Continue reinforcing I, II, III, and IV.

Kindergarten

I.   The adult's role is the crucial foundation and remains basically the same throughout all age levels (Chapter 7, pages 45-52 and pages 119-122).

II. Develop individual's understanding of feelings through Framework Activities (pages 122-124 and133-136 or pages 125-136 depending on students' level of understanding).

III. Develop vocabulary understanding relating to feelings and problem-solving (page 123).

IV. Introduce the Five-Step Process of "Say What's Wrong and Make It Right" incidentally as conflicts occur. (See pages 135-136 for "The Never Ending Lesson," a detailed description of *Introducing the Process Incidentally*.)

V. When the time is right for your class, (early in the school year) introduce the Five-Step Process of "Say What's Wrong and Make It Right" with the Formal Lesson Plan. (Appendix A, pages A 155-156, Intro and pages A162-175).

VI. Use the Target Lessons (pages 137-143) and the Active Listening Lesson (Appendix A, Pages A155-161) as follow-up and support of the students' mastery of the Five-Step Process.

VII. Continue reinforcing I, II, III, IV, V, and VI.

Primary and Upper

I.   The adult's role is the crucial foundation and remains the same throughout all age levels (Chapter 7, pages 45-52 and pages 119-122).

II, III,   Developing individual's understanding of feelings
& IV.   through Framework Activities (pages 122-124 and 133-136 or 125-136 depending on the students' level of understanding) and introducing the Five-Step Process of "Say What's Wrong and Make It Right" incidentally as conflicts occur. (See p. 135-136 for "The Never Ending Lesson," a detailed description of *Introducing the Process Incidentally*.)

V.   Introducing the Five-Step Process of "Say What's Wrong and Make It Right" with the Formal Lesson Plan (Appendix A, pages A155-156, Intro and pages A162-175) in the first few weeks of school.

VI.   Use the Target Lessons (pages 137-143) and the Active Listening Lesson (Appendix A, pages A155-161) as follow-up and support of the students' mastery of the Five-Step Process.

VII.   Continue reinforcing I, II, III, IV, V, and VI.

SAY WHAT'S WRONG AND MAKE IT RIGHT

"The Whole Truth"

A. Who was involved?_____

B. What was the problem? (You both must agree.)_____

_____

_____

C. Did you tell the other person you did not like what they were doing? ( )Yes ( ) No

D. Did you ask them to stop? ( )Yes ( )No

E. Did each of you say your feelings about the situation?_____

F. Did each of you listen to the other person's feelings? ( )Yes ( )No

G. What is the solution that you agreed upon?_____

_____

_____

H. When will you take action on the solution? (Date and Time)_____

Did you make a compromise? ( )Yes ( ) No

What are you both going to do to keep the peace?_____

_____

_____

I. How are you both feeling now?_____

_____

Student signatures: Date:_____

_____   _____

Parent Signature_____

196

Active Listening

1. Maintain Eye contact.

2. Listen! Do not talk.

3. Listen! Do not judge.

4. Listen! Do not offer advice or solutions.

5. Listen to repeat back.

6. Only ask questions to understand.

A COLLECTION OF STUDENT UPSETS IN THEIR WORDS

The following realistic scenarios are additional prompts for role-working (as described on pages 73–74).

Insert the correct subject: A classmate; brother; sister; parent; relative; friend.

1. Talking loud . . . Babbling . . . Going on and on . . . Singing . . . Tapping . . . Poking me when I am trying to do my work or listen to the teacher

2. Fighting . . . Arguing . . . Over games, who's out, who got the point, fouls . . . Being a sore loser . . . Throwing the ball out of reach when beaten

3. Not liking me . . . Saying I'm not wanted . . . Playing with others and leaving me out . . . Saying I can't do anything right

4. Taking things I'm using or playing with . . . Using my stuff . . . Ruining my stuff . . . Getting in my desk . . . Messing up my stuff and not cleaning it up

5. Name-calling . . . Teasing . . . Mimicking my friends or me

6. Blaming me for something I did not do . . . Not keeping a promise . . . Lying

7. Cussing . . . And they keep on saying bad words when I have asked them to stop.

8. Trying to con me into doing things I don't want to do . . . Crying or screaming to get their way

9. Being a know-it-all . . . saying "That's not how you do it" or "My way is better"

10. Interrupting my favorite TV program . . . Liking the tube better than me

11. Not stopping when asked to stop doing something they know bugs me

12. Not sharing things that belong to more than one person

ENDNOTES

CHAPTER 2

1. J. Cochran, N. Cochran, and E. Hatch, "Empathetic Communication for Conflict Resolution among Children," *The Person-Centered Journal*, 2002, http://adpca.org/journal/empathetic-communication-conflict-resolution-among-children.

CHAPTER 3

1. M.J. Elias and R.P. Weissberg, "Primary Prevention: Educational Approaches to Enhance Social and Emotional Learning," *The Journal of School Health*, May 2000, https://www.ncbi.nlm.nih.gov/pubmed/10900595.

2. Glenn and Nelsen's 2000 description of drawbacks to punishment in *Raising Self-Reliant Children in a Self-Indulgent World* (New York: Three Rivers Press, 2000), "Student Reaction to Punishment."

CHAPTER 4

1. Three of the texts I've cited in this book support this assertion: Goleman's *Emotional Intelligence;* Benson's, et. al's *What Kids Need to Succeed;* and Cummings's *Managing to Teach.*

CHAPTER 5

1. Betsy Brown Braun, *You're Not the Boss of Me* (New York: Harper, 2010).

CHAPTER 10

1. H. Stephen Glenn and Jane Nelsen, *Raising Self-Reliant Children in a Self-Indulgent World* (New York: Three Rivers Press, 2000).

2. Jane Nelsen, Lynn Lott, and H. Stephen Glenn, *Positive Discipline in the Classroom* (New York: Three Rivers Press, 2000).

3. H. Stephen Glenn and Jane Nelsen, *Raising Self-Reliant Children in a Self-Indulgent World* (New York: Three Rivers Press, 2000).

4. Daniel Goleman, *Emotional Intelligence* (New York: Bantam Books, 1995).

5. L. Browning, B. Davis, and V. Resta, "What Do You Mean 'Think Before I Act?'", *Journal of Research in Childhood*

Education, November 2009, https://www.tandfonline.com/doi/abs/10.1080/02568540009594766?journalCode=ujrc20.

6. C. Lewis, E. Schaps, and M. Watson, "The Caring Classroom's Edge," *Educational Leadership,* 1996.

7. Ruth Sidney Charney, *Teaching Children to Care* (Greenfield, MA: Northeast Foundation for Children, 1991).

8. Chris Byron, "Power, Politics, and the Middle School Classroom," *Democracy and Education,* 1999, https://files.eric.ed.gov/fulltext/ED433382.pdf.

9. Charney, *Teaching Children to Care.*

10. William Glasser, *Schools Without Failure* (New York: HarperCollins Publishers, 1975).

11. Nelsen, meanwhile, contends, "It is difficult for me to choose a favorite Positive Discipline parenting tool, but family meetings are at the top. Children learn so much during family meetings, such as listening, respecting differences, verbalizing appreciation, problem-solving, and experiencing that mistakes are wonderful opportunities to learn and focus on solutions." The source is Nelsen, Jane, <u>Positive Discipline Website</u> Blog, 11/05/2018.

BIBLIOGRAPHY

Benson, Peter L., Galbraith, Judy, and Espeland, Pamela. *What Kids Need to Succeed*. Minneapolis: Free Spirit Publishing, 1998.

Bluestein, Jane. *Creating Emotionally Safe Schools*. Deerfield Beach, FL: Health Communications, 2001.

Borba, Michele. *Esteem Builders*. Rolling Hills Estates, CA: Jalmar Press, 1989.

Borba, Michele. *Unselfie*. New York: Touchstone, 2016.

Braun, Betsy Brown. *You're Not the Boss of Me*. New York: Harper, 2010.

Briggs, Dorothy Corkille. *Your Child's Self-Esteem*. New York: Doubleday, 1975.

Browning, L., Davis, B., Resta, V. "What Do You Mean 'Think Before I Act?'" *Journal of Research in Childhood Education* 14 (2009): 232–238.

Byron, Christyne. "Power, Politics, and the Middle School Classroom." *Democracy and Education* 13 (1999): 23–27.

Canfield, Jack and Well, Harold C. *100 Ways to Enhance Self-concept in the Classroom.* Englewood Cliffs: Prentice Hall Curriculum and Teaching Series, 1976.

Charles, C. M. *Building Classroom Discipline.* New York: Longman, 1999.

Charles, C.M. *Building Classroom Discipline, Ninth Edition.* Boston: Pearson, 2008.

Charney, Ruth Sidney. *Teaching Children to Care.* Greenfield, MA: Northeast Foundation for Children, 1991.

Cochran, J., Cochran, N., and Hatch, E. "Empathetic Communication for Conflict Resolution among Children." *The Person-Centered Journal* 9, no. 2 (2002): 101–112.

The Conflict Manager Program: Peer Mediation for Elementary Schools. San Francisco: Community Boards, 2003.

Cummings, Carol. *Managing to Teach.* Edmonds, WA: Teaching, Inc., 1996.

BIBLIOGRAPHY

Curtis, Jamie Lee. *Today I Feel Silly & Other MOODS That Make My Day*. China: Joanna Cotler Books, 1998.

Dinkmeyer, Don and McKay, Gary D. *The Parent's Handbook: Systematic Training for Effective Parenting*. Circle Pines, MN: American Guidance Series, 1982.

Dougherty, M. "Designing Classroom Meetings for the Middle School Child." *The School Counselor* 28 (1980): 127–132.

Educators for Social Responsibility National Organization: www.esrnational.org.

Edwards, Dana and Mullis, Fran. "Classroom Meetings: Encouraging a Climate of Cooperation." *Professional School Counseling* 7, no. 1 (2003).

Elias, M.J. and Weissberg, R.P. "Primary Prevention: Educational Approaches to Enhance Social and Emotional Learning." *The Journal of School Health* 70 (2000): 186–190.

Epstein, Robert "What Makes a Good Parent" *Scientific American Mind* (Summer 2016).

Faber, Adele and Mazlish, Elaine. *How to Talk So Kids Can Learn*. New York: Fireside, 1995.

Faber, Adele and Mazlish, Elaine. *How to Talk So Kids Will Listen and Listen So Kids Will Talk*. New York: Rawson-Wade, 1980.

Fetsch, R.J. and Jacobson, B. "Manage Anger Through Family Meetings," *Fact Sheet 10.249*. Colorado State University Extension, April 2007.

Ginott, Haim. *Teacher and Child*. New York: Avon Books, 1975.

Glasser, William. *Schools Without Failure*. New York: HarperCollins Publishers, 1975.

Glenn, H. Stephen and Nelsen, Jane. *Raising Self-Reliant Children in a Self-Indulgent World*. New York: Three Rivers Press, 2000.

Goleman, Daniel. *Emotional Intelligence*. New York: Bantam Books, 1995.

Gordon, Thomas. *Parent Effectiveness Training*. New York: Three Rivers Press, 2000.

Hart, Sura and Hodson, Victoria Kindle. *The Compassionate Classroom*. La Crescenta, CA: Center for Nonviolent Communication, 2003.

Hannaford, Carla, *Smart Moves: Why Learning is Not All In Your Head*. Arlington, VA: Great Oceans Publishers, 1995.

Kashtan, Inbal. *Parenting from Your Heart*. Encinitas, CA: Puddle Dancer Press, 2003.

BIBLIOGRAPHY

Kohn, Alfie. *Beyond Discipline: From Compliance to Community*. Upper Saddle River, NJ: Merrill/ Prentice Hall, 2001.

Lewis, C., Schaps, E., and Watson, M. "The Caring Classroom's Edge." *Educational Leadership* 54 (1996): 16–21.

Nelsen, Jane. *Positive Discipline*. New York: Ballantine Books, 2006.

Nelsen, Jane, Lott, Lynn, and Glenn, H. Stephen. *Positive Discipline in the Classroom*. New York: Three Rivers Press, 2000.

Nelsen, J., Lott, L., and Glenn, H. Stephen. *Positive Discipline in the Classroom: A Teacher's Guide to Classroom Meetings*. Tulsa, OK: Empowering People Books, 1993.

Rosenberg, Marshall B. *Raising Children Compassionately*. Encinitas, CA: Puddle Dancer Press, 2003.

Shure, Myrna B., Geronimo, Di, and Foy, Theresa. *Raising a Thinking Child*. New York: Pocket Books, 1994.

Suskind, Ron. *Life, Animated*. Los Angeles: Kingswell, 2014.

Taylor, Karen. "Building Self-esteem Through Teaching Impact Self-Evaluation." Unpublished study presented to the Graduate Faculty of the School of Education, United States International University, Irvine, CA (1990).

Weiss, Ruth Palombo. "Emotion and Learning." *American Society for Training and Development* 54 (2000): 44–48.

Zakich, Rhea (2006) The Ungame (Talicor, Inc.: Plainwell, Michigan)

ACKNOWLEDGMENTS

"Say What's Wrong and Make It Right" (SWW&MIR) was developed as a joint venture. It evolved from my desire to develop self-discipline and independent problem-solving skills in children. My teaching partner, Deedee Carr, found the program so consistent with her own teaching goals that she joined in with enthusiasm. We came up with the foundation and framework, then honed the five-step process in our classroom with our students. Many of the materials are a result of our early experiences teaching the program. To this day, I find Deedee's input and support invaluable.

There are several others whose encouragement and guidance have been instrumental in the success and growth of "Say What's Wrong and Make It Right." Because of their gifts, I am deeply grateful to the following:

Julie Hume, for recognizing the value of SWW&MIR and creating the opportunity for it to be taught throughout Helen Estock School. It was through her continued insistence that I became a Mentor Teacher who taught the process throughout the Tustin Unified School District.

Marlys Blanc, A fellow educator in my early years of teaching, for introducing me to the important role that personal feelings play in understanding and solving problems. She introduced me to the concept that feelings are not right or wrong. Feelings are not good or bad. Feelings just are. This started me on the path that eventually led to the creation of "Say What's Wrong and Make it Right."

Christine Gregg, for her creative input and unwavering belief in SWW&MIR. She enriched the program and expanded my abilities as Mentor Teacher while she was serving as principal at Helen Estock School. As a principal in other schools, she also arranged for the SWW&MIR to be taught throughout her schools and to be continually reinforced.

Tustin Unified School District, for valuing the outcomes of the program and selecting me as Mentor Teacher for two years, which allowed for SWW&MIR to be taught to students, teachers, administrators, aides, and TUSD personnel staff.

Sally Warrick, for seeing the benefits of SWW&MIR, showing me how to influence a greater number of lives, and making the areas outside my comfort zone more comfortable.

Linda Pape, for teaching her students to SWW&MIR, arranging for the rest of her faculty to incorporate the program throughout their student body, and assisting in the teaching of the five-step process to Head Start teachers in Paradise Valley, Arizona.

Chuck Bleiker, for providing the opportunity for the preschool staff at the University of New Mexico and Head

ACKNOWLEDGMENTS

Start teachers at Florida International University to learn how to implement SWW&MIR with their students.

Cathy de Mayo, for her ongoing encouragement and editing skills.

Diane Fallon, for her support and suggestions.

Cathy Grothus and Carol Jones, for their coaching, their prodding, their editing, and for always being in my corner.

Renée Savant, for valuing and utilizing SWW&MIR in her family and as a classroom teacher. As an advocate of the program, her wisdom and continued support have urged me onward.

June Lee Pilsitz, for her research guidance.

Nancy Borden's students at Helen Estock School, Nathan Savant, and the Swann boys for their artistic contributions.

Brooke Warner and her staff at She Writes Press for their support and guidance, especially her editor, Krissa Lagos. She went through my manuscript with a fine-tooth comb, pointing out ways to make it technically consistent and giving me strategies to draw the reader in. She devoted her expertise to "Making It Right."

Cathy Gardner, for utilizing her computer skills to bring the manuscript to its final form.

My Writing Group—Christyne Byron, Deedee Carr, Kay Ferrell, Rosa Gaines, and sometimes Sheila Koff—for their honest editing, valuable writing skills, and unwavering encouragement of my goals with SWW&MIR. Without them this book might not be, and most certainly would not be what it is today.

All the educators, students, and parents who have taken this five-step process and made it their own. They have inspired and taught me on a daily basis with their modeling and their responses.

Charlie "Tex" Bleiker, my late husband, for advocating for this program in every way possible. He modeled and used it with his high school students. He shared it with the history teachers at Newport Harbor High School for their conflict resolution program. He used it in his personal life with his children, grandchildren, and me, his mate. Equally as important, Charlie understood my need to spend countless hours to improve and share SWW&MIR. He was an objective sounding board and critic, and gave me undying emotional sustenance.

ABOUT THE AUTHOR

The program creator and author of this book, Karen Taylor-Bleiker, MA in Person-Centered Education, has delighted in the results from sharing this process. She has trained students, principals, teachers, staff, counselors, youth workers, and parents in communication and problem-solving skills in preschools, elementary schools, and the Orange County Department of Education. During that same period, she presented and trained at universities and leadership conferences in Southern California, Arizona, New Mexico, and Florida.

Made in the USA
Columbia, SC
31 October 2019

82475157R00126